THE WRITER'S COMPANION
A SHORT HANDBOOK

THE WRITER'S COMPANION

A SHORT HANDBOOK

William H. Roberts
University of Lowell

Little, Brown and Company
Boston   Toronto

For My Father and
For Patsy

Library of Congress Cataloging in Publication Data

Roberts, William H. (William Howell)
　The writer's companion.

　Includes index.
　1. English language—Grammar—1950–
　2. English language—Rhetoric. I. Title.
　PE1112.R566　1984　　　808'.042　　　84-20136
　ISBN 0-316-74988-5

Copyright © 1985 by William H. Roberts

All rights reserved. No part of this book may be reproduced in any form or by any electronic or mechanical means including information storage and retrieval systems without permission in writing from the publisher, except by a reviewer who may quote brief passages in a review.

Library of Congress Catalog Card No. 84-20136

ISBN 0-316-74988-5

9 8 7 6 5 4 3 2 1

MV

Published simultaneously in Canada
by Little, Brown & Company (Canada) Limited

Printed in the United States of America

Credits

Page 8. "Garfield Is a Star." Copyright © 1984 by Naomi P. Claggett. Used by permission.

Page 15. "The Birth of an Outdoorsman." Copyright © 1984 by Joel Vincent. Used by permission.

Page 118. From "Stopping by Woods on a Snowy Evening" from *The Poetry of Robert Frost* edited by Edward Connery Lathem. Copyright

(continued on page 246)

Preface

To the Instructor

The Writer's Companion: A Short Handbook offers students a clear and concise reference guide to improving writing skills for class, for research, and for the job. It is designed to function as a companion for independent student use by providing clear explanations of common writing problems. The most substantial portion of the book discusses these common problems alphabetically by correction symbol, and *The Writer's Companion* is cross-referenced throughout.

Although the book is designed for independent student reference, it can also be used as a classroom text. Part 1 previews the writing process as it moves rapidly and clearly from prewriting to revision. Two corrected model student papers are included to introduce students to part of the revision process and to demonstrate how they can use the book independently. This section also enables you to share your expectations about writing with your students. Part 2 presents a succinct review of grammar that can be studied in class or independently. Part 3 is an alphabetical presentation of concise discussions of forty-five common student writing problems. Each of these discussions contains exercises that can be used independently or in class for common problems. Part 4 is a comprehensive step-by-step guide to writing the research paper. The fully annotated model paper on "Death and Dying in America" follows the 1984 revised MLA guidelines for documentation.

In preparing *The Writer's Companion* I have kept the principle of student reference in mind, not filling the book with unnecessary detail. The tone is positive and friendly to encourage student use, and the content is devoted to the basic fundamentals of successful writing.

To the Student

The fundamental purpose of *The Writer's Companion* is to provide you with a book that you will want to use because it is easy to use. It is written to provide you with clear discussions and brief answers to the most frequently asked questions about writing. Quick and easy reference determined the organization of this short handbook. To achieve this end, the book has been divided into four parts.

1. Part 1 is a brief discussion of the writing process followed by two papers written by college freshmen and marked and commented on by their instructors. It would be useful to read this chapter carefully with your instructor for two reasons: (a) You can learn a lot about your instructor's expectations by discussing the model papers, and (b) you can learn how to use *The Writer's Companion* by doing the revision exercise that follows the student papers.
2. Part 2, a review of basic grammar, defines the terms that you and your instructor will need to share in order to talk meaningfully about writing.
3. Part 3 is the heart and soul of *The Writer's Companion*. It is an alphabetical discussion of forty-five of the most persistent student writing problems. There is no complicated letter-and-number code reference system. The forty-five sections are alphabetized by correction symbol to aid your independent reference. The discussions are clear and concise, and each is followed by at least one exercise for use in or out of class.
4. Part 4 is a comprehensive discussion of writing a research paper. The commentary on the model research paper should assist you in writing such a paper.

As its title suggests, *The Writer's Companion: A Short Handbook* is brief and friendly. It is easy to use, and it includes clear answers to the questions that you are most likely to ask about writing.

Acknowledgements

I wish to thank my colleagues and students at the University of Lowell. Special thanks go to William Burto, Arthur Friedman, Joe Zaitchik, and Greg Turgeon. I also wish to thank all of the professionals at Little, Brown and Company, but especially Molly Faulkner, Joe Opiela, Allison Hoover, and Linda Belamarich. A special thanks goes to Sally Stickney, my production editor, who patiently taught me how books are made. In addition, I wish to thank Professor Richard Beal for his encouragement at the early stages, and David Skwire, of Cuyahoga Community College, Melinda Kramer, of Purdue University, Jane Haynes, of Ball State University, Paul Bryant, of Colorado State University, Maureen Goldman, of Bentley College, C. Jeriel Howard, of Northeastern Illinois University, and Randall Popken, of the University of Kansas, for their constructive comments on the developing manuscript.

WHR

Contents

1 Using this Book to Write Better Essays   1

Prewriting   1
   From topic to thesis   2
   Purpose   5
   Audience   5

Writing the Essay   6

A Ten-Step Checklist to a Complete Essay   6

Model Essays   7

2 A Concise Review of Grammar   19

Parts of Speech   19
   Nouns   20
   Pronouns   21
   Verbs   23
   Adjectives   24
   Adverbs   26
   Prepositions   27
   Conjunctions   28
   Articles   30
   Interjections   30

Sentences 31
    Subjects 32
    Predicates 33
    Complements 33
    Phrases 34
    Clauses 36
    Sentence types 38

3 An Alphabetical List of Frequent Writing Problems 41

1 Abbreviations 41
    Titles 41
    Technical terms 42
    Time 42
    Familiar names 42
    Foreign phrases 43
    Currency and percentages 43
    Other titles 43
    Units of measure 44
    Geographical names 44
    Days, months, and holidays 44
    School courses 44
    Common words 44
    Elements of official names 44

2 Misuse of Adjectives and Adverbs 45
    Linking verbs and modifiers 46
    Comparisons 46
    Irregular forms 47

Contents

3 Errors in Subject and Verb Agreement 49
Compound subjects 50
Indefinite pronouns 51
Collective nouns 52
Nouns plural in form only 52
Inverted word order 52
Nouns and pronouns between the subject and verb 52
Linking verbs 53
Titles 53
Nouns of time, money, weight, and measurement 53
Relative pronouns as subjects 53

4 Errors in Case Form 54
Subjective case forms 54
Objective case forms 55
Possessive case forms 55
Compound constructions 56
We and us constructions 56
Appositives 57
Than or as 57
Who and whom 57

5 Capitalization and Lower Case Form 59
Titles 59
Proper nouns and proper adjectives 59
Honorary and official titles 61
Specific school courses 61
Relations 61
Trade names 62
Abbreviations 62

    Directions   62
    Exceptions   62

6 Cliches   64

7 Faulty Coordination   65
    Coordination of unrelated ideas   66
    Excessive coordination   66

8 Comma Splices   68

9 Diction   70
    Current and general use   71
    Reputable use   72
    Denotation and connotation   74
    Be concise   75

10 Dangling Modifiers   76

11 Sentence Fragments   78
    Appositive phrases   78
    Prepositional phrases   78
    Infinitive phrases   79
    Participial phrases   79
    Dependent clauses   79
    Objective clauses   80
    Subject with no complete verb   80
    Permissible fragments   80

12 Fused or Run-On Sentences   82

13 Uses of the Hyphen   83
    Compound expressions   84
    Fractions and compound numbers   84

Word division 84
Preventing ambiguity 85

14 Italics (Underlining) 85
Titles 85
Names of vehicles 86
Foreign words and expressions 86
Words, numbers, and figures 87
Emphasis 87

15 Faulty Logic 88
Establishing a moderate tone 88
Supporting opinions with facts 88
Oversimplification 88
Hasty generalizations 88
Post hoc 89
Non sequitur 89
False analogy 90
Stereotypes 90
Ad hominem 90

16 Misplaced modifiers 91
Prepositional phrases and subordinate clauses 92
Limiting adverbs 92
Ambiguous (squinting) modifiers 93

17 Manuscript Form 94
Typed papers 94
Handwritten papers 95
Proofreading and corrections 95

18 Errors in the Use of Numbers 96

19 Faulty Parallelism 97

20 Uses of the Period 99
    Ends of sentences 99
    Mild commands and indirect questions 99
    Abbreviations 99
    Quotation marks 100

21 Uses of the Question Mark 100
    Direct questions 100
    Quotation marks 101
    Parentheses 101

22 Uses of the Exclamation Point 101

23 Uses of the Comma 102
    Independent clauses 102
    Elements in a series 103
    Coordinate adjectives 103
    Introductory elements 104
    Nonrestrictive modifiers and appositives 105
    Parenthetic elements and transitional words 106
    Mild interjections and direct address 106
    Absolute phrases 107
    Dates, addresses, letter forms, and long numbers 107
    Quotations 108

24 Uses of the Semicolon 109
    Independent clauses 109
    Conjunctive adverbs 110
    Long and complex clauses 110
    Items in a series 110

25 Uses of the Colon   112
Lists of appositives   112
Formal quotations   112
Explanations   112
Business letters   113
Titles and subtitles   113
Other uses   113

26 Uses of the Dash   113
Interruptions and parenthetic elements   114
Summary statements   114
Introductory substantives   114

27 Uses of Parentheses and Brackets   115
Parentheses   115
Brackets   116

28 Uses of Quotation Marks   117
Direct quotations   117
Long quotations   118
Dialogue, poetry, and lengthy prose passages   118
Quotations within quotations   119
Titles   119
Words used in special or ironical senses   119
Quotation marks used with other marks of punctuation   120

29 Uses of the Apostrophe   121
Possessive case forms   121
Contractions   123
Plurals of letters and numbers   123

30 Uses of the Ellipsis Mark and the Slash 124
Ellipsis mark 124
Slash 125

31 Paragraphs 127

32 Paragraph Unity 127

33 Paragraph Coherence 131

34 Paragraph Development 133

35 Introductory and Concluding Paragraphs 137

36 Ineffective Use of the Passive Voice 140

37 Errors in the Use of Pronouns: Reference and Agreement 142
Agreement of pronouns 142
Singular antecedents 142
Agreement of indefinite pronouns 143
Reference of pronouns 144

38 Spelling 147
Proofread 147
Develop special "tricks" 147
Learn spelling rules 148
Do not rely on pronunciation 150
Make a list 151
Spelling of foreign plurals 151
Study the components of words 152

39 Faulty Subordination 153

40 Errors in Verb Tense   156

41 Thesis Sentences   158

42 Using Transitions   161
    Transitional words and phrases   161
    Pronoun reference   161
    Repetition of key terms   161
    Parallelism   161

43 Glossary of Usage   162

44 Sentence Variety   169

45 Wordy — Unnecessary Repetition   172

4 Writing the Research Paper   177

Defining the Research Paper   177

Choosing a Topic   178

Researching the Topic   180
    Prepare a working bibliography   180
    Judge the sources   182
    Prepare a tentative thesis and outline   183
    Take notes on the sources   185
    Work carefully to avoid plagiarism   187

Composing a Formal Outline   188

Writing the First Draft   190

Preparing the Final Draft   197

Preparing the Works Cited Page   198
    Abbreviations   198
    Missing data   199
    Two or more works by the same author   199
    Books   199
    Periodicals, magazines, and newspapers   202
    Other sources   203

A Sample Research Paper   206

Index   247

1
Using this Book to Write Better Essays

Most of the essays assigned in your college writing classes will be five to seven hundred words long. Each essay will consist of four or five paragraphs: an introductory paragraph, three or four paragraphs in the body of the essay, and a concluding statement or paragraph. The essays that you write will be nonfiction compositions in which you present your views by analyzing and interpreting your topic.

PREWRITING

Writing is a more rewarding experience if you think carefully about the topic before you begin to write. Too many students simply begin writing without thinking first, and, as a result, their writing lacks careful development and clear organization. The process in which you discover what you think and feel about your topic is called *prewriting*. Prewriting includes the thinking, researching, and reading that you do before you begin the first draft, and its purpose is to allow you to find a focus for your topic.

Before you begin to write, you should ask yourself three questions:

1. What am I going to write about? [topic]
2. What is my purpose for writing? [purpose]
3. Who will be reading my essay? [audience]

From topic to thesis

Usually you will be allowed to choose a topic from a list of suggestions. You should focus on a subject that interests you as soon as possible, allowing yourself ample time to think about the subject. If you want to convince others that what you say is worth reading, you must be enthusiastic and well-informed about your topic. Don't write about what you think your instructor wants to hear; write about what you want your audience to hear.

Frequently you will be assigned general subject areas to write about that will need to be narrowed down to a topic that can be fully developed within your word limit. For example, you may be asked to write on such broad issues as parenting, high school and college, marriage, professional sports, or the energy problem. Let's say, for example, that you decide to write on the energy problem. Clearly this topic is too broad to discuss in four or five paragraphs. Perhaps you could limit it by discussing what your family is doing to save energy. Now you have a topic. The next step is to jot down rapidly every idea that you can think of relating to the topic. Think of this as a list — it is not a formal outline. Once you have completed your list (or random outline) you must convert your topic into a thesis to focus your essay and to prepare the reader for its content. (See Thesis Sentences, p. 158.)

The *thesis sentence* is a sentence that states the central idea of your essay, and usually it is expressed clearly in the opening paragraph. The thesis sentence should be specific and concise because it keeps the writer focused as the essay is developed and prepares the reader for the essay's content. While a topic merely announces what you are going to write about, a thesis sentence should make an assertion about your topic that reveals your attitude about your subject. Also, the thesis sentence often provides the reader with an indication of how you plan to organize the main ideas within your essay. The assertion made in the thesis sentence, then, defines the job of the rest of the essay, which is to support that assertion. Notice the differences between the topic and thesis here:

TOPIC
What my family is doing to reduce heating costs.

THESIS

My family has worked hard to fight the high cost of home heating by purchasing a woodburning stove, increasing the amount of insulation, and installing storm windows and doors.

Now you are ready to begin thinking seriously about the content of your essay. At the same time that you begin to develop your thesis, you must also be thinking about your *purpose* and your *audience* (see pp. 5–6). Let's consider the development of the thesis first. The thesis statement in the above example suggests to your readers that you plan to discuss the energy problem by examining three measures your family has taken to fight the high cost of heating. (In other words, you have suggested an organizational pattern that your readers will expect you to follow.)

1. Woodburning stove
2. Increased insulation
3. Storm windows and doors

Each of these topics probably will be developed in a separate paragraph, and when you join the paragraphs together, you will have a unified and coherent essay of four or five paragraphs. (See pp. 127–133 for a discussion of paragraph unity and coherence.)

You are now ready to prepare a topic outline in which you use the above topics as the major divisions and add subdivisions for each so that your paragraphs will be developed. Frequently each of the major divisions in the outline represents a paragraph in the paper. Here is an outline showing how this topic will be developed.

    I. Introduction — including thesis statement (See Introductory and Concluding Paragraphs, p. 137.)

        My family has worked hard to fight the high cost of home heating by purchasing a woodburning stove, increasing the amount of insulation, and installing storm windows and doors.

    II. Three years ago my father installed a woodburning stove in our family room.

  A. Initial cost of stove and wood
  B. Installation and maintenance
    1. Installed stove into fireplace opening ourselves
    2. Maintained stove with chimney and stove brushes ourselves
III. Last year we added insulation and caulking compound.
  A. Insulation
    1. Attic floor
    2. Basement ceiling
  B. Caulking compound and other weatherproof materials
    1. Windows and doors
    2. Electrical outlets
IV. This year we added storm windows and doors.
  A. Windows
    1. Three-way aluminum
    2. Custom-made and caulked
  B. Doors
    1. Wooden front door
    2. Metal sliding patio storm door
V. Conclusion (See Introductory and Concluding Paragraphs, p. 137.)
  Estimate of total savings

  Many students feel uncomfortable using a formal outline for shorter papers. The complicated format with its major and subordinate parts bothers them. When composing shorter papers, some students often feel more comfortable with a "rough" or "scratch" outline. A "scratch" outline simply lists the topics to be developed in the most effective order. Here is a possible "scratch" outline for this assignment.

  Ways my family has fought the high cost of home heating
  Woodburning stove — cost and installation
  Insulation of attic floor and basement ceiling
  Caulking
  Storm windows and doors
  Estimate of total savings

If you feel more comfortable with such an outline, use this form.

Prewriting

The purpose of an outline is to give the general shape of your composition. It should serve as a guide that helps the writer remember the major topics and to see if movement from topic to topic is clear and logical.

Purpose

As soon as you have chosen your topic, you should also think about why you are writing this essay. Are you, for example, planning to entertain, to persuade, or to inform your readers? As you plan your thesis and examine the items in your random outline, you will be deciding which rhetorical approach to use. You need to determine whether your paper will be primarily narration, argument, description, or exposition.

Rarely, however, will you use only one rhetorical approach. Most often one approach will be predominant, but others may be used. With the above topic on home energy savings, for example, you will rely primarily on explanation (exposition). That is, you will explain how your family has saved money and energy. It is likely that you may also want to persuade your readers to take similar steps. You may also describe how you installed your wood-burning stove: this approach could be either description or narration. The important point to remember as you plan your essay is that your fundamental purpose is to explain.

Audience

Writers do not express themselves in a vacuum. Since writers write to readers, they must have an audience in mind. Although you are writing for the instructor who assigned the essay and who will evaluate it, do not try to write solely for your instructor. Doing so often makes your language sound unnatural and your content contrived because you are trying to write what you think your instructor wants to hear rather than what you want to say. Try instead to choose an audience with whom you might actually communicate. Unless you can pinpoint a specific audience like the editor of your student newspaper, the mayor of your home town, or an employer, you should write to a general audience — an audience that you may assume shares your interests and is reasonably serious and thoughtful about what you have to say. For example, people who are interested in reducing home heating costs would be the audience for the topic in the example discussed earlier.

During the prewriting process, think carefully about your purpose and audience. Each of these factors will determine what your thesis sentence will say and how it will be developed in your essay. You are now ready to begin writing the rough draft.

WRITING THE ESSAY

Now that you have completed the prewriting steps and your thesis and outline are in front of you, writing the first draft should be a much less threatening task. When writing a first draft, you should try to get your ideas on paper rapidly. Don't worry about mechanical errors; you can correct them later. Think about getting your ideas on the page as rapidly as possible, and then stop writing. You should keep thinking, but put the first draft aside. When you come back to it a day or two later, you may have fresh ideas to add. You will also be far enough from the original draft that you can be objective and look at it from the perspective of a critical reader. As you revise the first draft, you should go over your paper with the greatest care. The final draft must be as clean and direct and as free from errors as you can make it. If you become familiar with and avoid the writing problems discussed in Part 3, you will have taken a major step towards the preparation of a polished final draft.

A TEN-STEP CHECKLIST TO A COMPLETE ESSAY

1. Select a topic, think about it, and gather some information.
2. Make a list of random ideas that relate to your topic — do this rapidly.
3. From the above list determine your response to your topic — how you plan to approach it. Do your ideas fall into patterns?
4. Convert the topic to a thesis sentence.
5. Prepare a topic outline that develops your thesis. As you do this, think about purpose and audience.

Model Essays

6. Write the first draft rapidly. At this early stage content is most important. Then put the first draft aside for a day or two.
7. Revise and change the first draft as necessary.
8. Type the final manuscript. (See Manuscript Form, p. 94.)
9. Read carefully and respond to your instructor's corrections and suggestions.
10. Revise or rewrite the final manuscript.

EXERCISE

1. Choose three of the general subjects below. Think about each topic and how you might approach it. Jot down these ideas. Convert each topic to a thesis sentence that will be used in an essay of five to seven hundred words.

   admission to college   the environment
   rock music   conserving energy
   professional sports   marriage
   movies   humor
   television   automobiles
   travel   periodicals

2. Choose one of the three topics that you converted to a thesis sentence and make a topic outline. (Your instructor may suggest that you complete the essay from this outline.)

MODEL ESSAYS

Here are two student essays that an instructor has corrected using the correction symbols explained in Part 3. Your instructor probably will go over the first essay with you carefully, showing you how to use this book as a reference to help you prepare and revise your own essays and to help you understand how to respond to the corrections and comments that he or she makes. (Part 3 contains a detailed discussion of each of the corrections and comments in the following essay.) You will need to go over the second essay yourself to reinforce the points that your instructor emphasized with the first essay.

Garfield Is a Star

Garfield, if you haven't read the funny papers lately, is a cat. To know that he has acheived star status, just pick up the Sunday Globe; the first thing you'll see is Garfield's full color leer. He has top billing these days.

Garfield has been embraced by his fans partly because he is a cat and partly because he is all too failingly human. Cats are popular these days, and more people have come to appreciate those notable feline traits of superiority, condescension, and chutzpah. Garfield has these and more. See how he handles Odie, the dog who is drawn as a cat's-eye view of a dog, all flapping appendages and dripping tongue. Odie has just made Garfield fall head first into his food dish with a surprise bark from behind. "I really envy you, Odie" says Garfield seizing him by the neck, "Imagine, the first house-pet on the moon" and up goes Odie with a POW! It's the sort of thing my cat would do if he could.

Garfield often gets away with things we wish we could. Displaying a laid-back careless attitude and never showing guilt or regret. Jon, his owner, is forever putting him on a diet, but being fat hasn't bothered him yet. "Hark! Isn't that the sound of a lasagna noodle being placed on a bed of ricotta cheese?" asks Garfield while Jon is doing his best to cook in secret. "The secret of dieting with no discomfort," asserts a supine Garfield another day, is "don't move a muscle, eat no calories, burn no calories."

Garfield is funny even to look at. He and his supporting cast all have eyes like ping-pong balls that protrude quite naturally from their somewhat improbable bodies. Jim Davis, Garfield's creator, manages to paint a full range of expression on those bulbous orbs. When Garfield's eyes are shut in blissful contentment, the reader shares his comfort. Garfield's body is short and pudgy, totally lacking in classic feline grace. He doesn't appear to get any more exercise than a stroll from bed to dish. Indeed, as you follow his adventures, you'll discover that is essentially the case. The only time he ever caught a mouse, he and the mouse had arranged a chase as a charade. Garfield generally sports a smirk reminiscent of a certain actor who thought anyone who hated kids and dogs couldn't be all bad. I think Garfield would agree. When his caterwauling earns him a bonk on the head, his reply of "Obviously sir, you are not a patron of the arts" is delivered in best W. C. Fields' style.

    The character of Garfield that we love and laugh at came across well in a recent strip where Jon holds Garfield affectionately and muses, "What's so special about a pet-owner relationship, Garfield? Could it be everyone needs someone to lord over?"

    "Could be," answers Garfield, "but what do you get out of it?"

Your instructor will probably write a comment at the end of your paper in addition to the correction symbols written in the margins. As you revise and respond to your instructor's comments, you must take both the correction symbols and the comments into consideration. The comment on the Garfield essay might look something like this:

> *This essay is full of crisp details and specific examples, and it does more than describe — it analyzes. The ideas are tightly grouped, and all of the pieces fit together, contributing to a unified whole. However, the introductory paragraph should state the topic more explicitly in a thesis sentence. The wording is lively, but many mechanical problems detract from the presentation. This will be an effective piece of writing if you revise carefully.*

This student should be pleased with much of the instructor's response to "Garfield Is a Star." The major areas of development and organization are quite acceptable, except that a concrete thesis sentence is needed in the introductory paragraph. Otherwise, the paragraphs are well-developed and fit together tightly, leading to a concluding quotation that highlights the central points of the essay. Clearly, then, the major problems with this essay are at the sentence level as shown by the correction symbols in the margin.

You will note that each of these correction symbols is explained in Part 3 where they are presented alphabetically. Now let's discuss each of the symbols used to correct this essay to demonstrate how you can use this book to your advantage when you revise your own essays and respond to your instructor's comments.

Line 1 — (ts) Thesis Sentences, see p. 158. A thesis sentence should do more than announce the topic (as this student has done). It should also establish a clear focus and perhaps indicate how the main ideas of the essay are organized. The writer may wish to end the opening paragraph with a thesis sentence mentioning the three major points that are developed about Garfield. As now written, the opening sentence announces the topic and catches our interest, but it also needs a clear focus. One possible thesis sentence for this essay is:

> Garfield appeals to us because we delight in the dual personality of a cat and a human, and we laugh at his absurd appearance.

This sentence tells the reader that the essay will discuss three points:

1. Garfield's personality as a cat
2. Garfield's personality as a human
3. Garfield's absurd appearance

Line 2 — (**sp**) Spelling, see p. 147. This spelling error should have been detected as the writer was polishing the essay. Writers must use their dictionaries. The spelling rule that was violated is the *i* before *e* rule (see p. 149).

Line 4 — (**hy**) Uses of the Hyphen, see p. 83. The hyphen should be used to form compound words. Two or more words used as a single adjective before a noun are usually hyphenated. This rule is discussed in Uses of the Hyphen, p. 84.

Line 6 — (**pas**) Ineffective Use of the Passive Voice, see p. 140. Generally, the passive voice adds unnecessary words and tends to be less specific. There are situations, however, when the passive voice should be used. One such situation is when it is more important to emphasize the receiver of the action than the doer. This sentence in the essay is better than its active counterpart:

> Fans embrace Garfield partly because he is a cat. . . .

The author prefers the passive voice in this situation. Others may not. Perhaps the best solution would be to rewrite the sentence another way using the active voice:

> Garfield's fans embrace him partly because he is a cat. . . .

Line 11 — (**var**) Sentence Variety, see p. 169. This comment commends the writer for varying the sentence structure. The short,

Model Essays

simple sentence "Garfield has these and more" is emphatic because it contrasts structurally with the longer sentences that precede and follow it.

Line 15 — (**mm**) Misplaced Modifiers, see p. 91. This sentence is ambiguous because the modifier "with a surprise bark from behind" is not as close to the noun it modifies (Odie) as it should be. Corrected, the sentence is clear:

> Odie, with a surprise bark from behind, has just made Garfield fall head first into his food dish.

Line 17 — (**p/,**) Uses of the Comma, see p. 102. "Seizing him by the neck" is a nonrestrictive modifier; that is, it is not essential to the meaning of the sentence. A nonrestrictive modifier should be set off by commas (see Uses of the Comma, p. 105).

Lines 22–23 — (**frag**) Sentence Fragments, see p. 78. A sentence fragment usually occurs when you treat a dependent clause or phrase as if it were a complete sentence. "Displaying a laid-back careless attitude and never showing guilt or regret" is a participial phrase modifying the proper noun Garfield. (See the section on participial phrases, p. 79.) This fragment could be corrected as follows:

> Garfield, displaying a laid-back careless attitude and never showing guilt or fear, often gets away with things we wish we could.

If you are having difficulty writing complete sentences, you should carefully read the section on sentence fragments, pp. 78–82, and do the exercise at the end.

Line 24 — (**ref**) Errors in the Use of Pronouns: Reference and Agreement, see p. 142. Pronouns do not have meaning themselves but derive their meaning from the nouns they replace. A pronoun must refer only to one antecedent. (See Reference of pronouns, p. 144.) In the sentence in question, the pronoun *him* presents a problem. Does *him* refer to Jon or Garfield? The sentence should be revised in this manner:

> Jon, his owner, is forever putting him on a diet, but being fat hasn't bothered Garfield yet.

Lines 33–34 — (**d/dic**) Diction, see p. 70. Correct diction means the accurate choice of a word or words to express an idea. Here the reader commends the student for using words that are precise and sharp — "eyes like ping-pong balls that protrude . . ."

Lines 42–43 — (**w/rep**) Wordy — Unnecessary Repetition, see p. 172. Writers tend to use more words than necessary. Good writing should be precise and concise. As part of the revision process, writers should eliminate words, phrases, and even sentences that are empty or needlessly repetitious. The sentence that begins "Indeed, as you follow his adventures . . ." adds nothing to the development of the paragraph. In fact, the paragraph is better without it.

Line 46 — (**d/dic**) Diction, see p. 70. The phrase "of a certain actor" is vague. Although it becomes clear that the writer is referring to W. C. Fields, there is no reason for making the reader work unnecessarily. Why not rewrite the sentence with a more precise reference?

> Garfield generally sports a smirk reminiscent of W. C. Fields who said, "Anyone who hates kids and dogs can't be all bad."

Line 49 — (**pas**) Ineffective Use of the Passive Voice, see p. 140. Unlike the discussion of the passive voice in line 6 above, there is little justification for this passive construction. This use of the passive voice is unnecessarily wordy, and it places the emphasis on W. C. Fields rather than on what he said. Here is a possible revision:

> When his caterwauling earns him a bonk on the head, Garfield replies in his best W. C. Fields style, "Obviously sir, you are not a patron of the arts."

Line 54 — (t) Errors in Verb Tense, see p. 156. Writers should not mix tenses. There is no apparent reason here to shift from the present tense to the past. Use *comes* across.

Lines 58–59 — (¶ **intro**) Introductory and Concluding Paragraphs, see p. 137. Here the writer is being commended for an effective conclusion. The quotation captures the mood of the essay, and, at the same time, it makes clear that the writer is bringing the essay to a close.

EXERCISE

Read the following student essay and study the correction symbols in the margin and the instructor's comment at the end. A list of the correction symbols used in this essay follows the instructor's comment. Study the discussion of each of the errors in Part 3 and revise the essay accordingly. Be prepared to discuss the reasons for the revisions.

The Birth of an Outdoorsman

pas   My decision to hike the Appalachian Trail (had been made) last January when my cousin, Andrew Alston, a Tennessean and outdoorsman in the tradition of Davy Crockett, was visiting us for the New Year's holiday. He spent most of his   5 visit trying to coax me into joining him on what he referred to as a "summer ramble" from the Great Smokey Mountains of Tennessee to the Berkshires of Western Massachusetts. When I relented just one

p ↑   day before Andy was to return (home he) was ecstatic.   10

w/rep   That night we (compiled a list) of the essential

gear our journey would require and we worked out the details necessary for an 1100 mile hike. Andy left the next morning with my promise to join him in Tennessee on the fourteenth of July. Through June and early July I worked in Boston at my father's printing company. Weekends (were spent) at home on Cape Cod breaking in my gear and preparing my body for the rigors of overland hiking by trudging over the soft sand and dunes of the Cape. As arranged, I flew to Knoxville and met Andy on July 14. On the ride to his hometown of Gatlinburg, a small town at the western foot of the Smokies, I pronounced myself fit and eager to start our journey. We were asleep by nine that night, and on our way by six the next morning.

The first few days our pace was fast and my inexperience was obvious as I learned that hiking the rugged Appalachian Trail was not like my training routine on a level Cape Cod. A slight ankle sprain taught me not to stray from the trail unless necessary. The first few nights (were spent) taping my ankle, soothing my blisters, and discarding the (non-essentials) that I had added to my list in Andy's absence. Through all my suffering, Andy was an

understanding and enthusiastic companion. The more
I hurt, the more he encouraged me onward.

The following weeks were just the reverse of
the first. With each passing day my blisters
diminished and my pack lightened. Gradually I became more aware of the bounty and beauty of America. Through Tennessee, Virginia, Pennsylvania, and New York: through the Great Smokies, the Blue Ridge Mountains, and the Kittatinnies. Andy introduced me to his special world. The
mountains, the miles, and weeks passed all too
quickly. On September 1 we rendezvoused with my
father in North Adams, Massachusetts, and then
spent the last few days of summer on Cape Cod.

Three months have passed since my first
ramble: three months to trek the cool mountains
of the mid-Atlantic states; three months to smell
the luxuriant blooms of southern serviceberry,
redbud, and sourwood. Three months have passed
since the hike that taught me to understand
what the Massachusetts naturalist Benton MacKaye
meant when he said, "To walk. To see. To see
what you see".

> *The many precise details that you use give this essay a vivid tone and specific voice. The opening paragraph is somewhat deceptive. You lead your readers to believe that the essay will be about the hike itself. In actuality, the essay is more about preparations for the hike and the triumph of its completion. You should limit your focus in the opening and develop the paper accordingly. Begin your revision by correcting the mechanical errors.*

Reread the directions that precede the student essay and revise the items below.

1. Line 1 — (**pas**)
2. Line 10 — (**p/,**)
3. Line 11 — (**w/rep**)
4. Line 12 — (**RO**)
5. Line 15 — (**¶**)
6. Line 17 — (**pas**)
7. Line 25 — (**no p/,**)
8. Line 32 — (**pas**)
9. Line 34 — (**hy**)
10. Line 43 — (**cap**)
11. Line 42 — (**frag**)
12. Line 53 — (**good paral**)
13. Line 57 — (**p/ " "**)

2
A Concise Review of Grammar

Since this reference book addresses problems writers most frequently encounter, here is a concise review of grammar to reacquaint you with some of the basic grammatical terms that you need to know in order to write accurately and to use this book efficiently. For most of us, the study of basic grammar is a means to an end because we already follow most of the conventions of English without really thinking about them. Some errors will occur, however, and a familiarity with the rules makes the correction of those errors less of a problem. A knowledge of grammar can help you improve your writing by showing you how language works. Moreover, it will also provide you and your instructor with the common vocabulary used to evaluate your writing.

PARTS OF SPEECH

Traditionally words are classified into groups called *parts of speech*. These groups are determined by the *form* of the words and the *function* that they perform in a sentence. The parts of speech in English are noun, pronoun, verb, adjective, adverb, preposition, conjunction, determiner, and interjection. The first five (noun, pronoun, verb, adjective, and adverb) are identified by the position they occupy within a sentence and by their form — the inflectional endings. The last four (preposition, conjunction, determiner, and interjection) are identified by their function. They do not have inflectional endings, and they are identified most readily by their use and position relative to other words in the sentence.

Consider the following sentence:

The glooby gorks burgled in the borgs.

We know that *borgs* is a noun without knowing its dictionary meaning. We know this because of its form and position. It has a plural ending, and it follows two structure words — the preposition *in,* and the article (determiner) *the.* We know *in* is a preposition because we recognize its position relative to the noun, *borgs,* and the verb, *burgled.*

Many words, however, can serve as more than one part of speech. The word *walk,* for example, can be a noun:

The *walk* through the swamp was wet.

Or it can be a verb:

The wardens *walk* up the corridor hourly.

Nouns

In addition to determining nouns by form, as in *borgs* above, most of you have learned that a noun names something. Nouns can name something tangible like a person, a place, or an object (*Mary, London, computer*); or they can name something intangible like an idea (*devotion, success, pride*).

Most nouns are recognizable because they add an *-s* or *-es* to form the plural (*student, students; glass, glasses*). Most nouns also show possession by adding an apostrophe and an *-s* (the *child's* alligator). There are some nouns, however, that do not usually form plurals. Mass nouns such as *salt* and *gold* and abstract nouns such as *anger* and *wisdom* are of this group.

Many nouns can be preceded by determiners, *a, an, the;* or by words showing possession, *my, your, Gary's*. These structure words are helpful because they announce the presence of a noun.

Proper nouns name specific people, places, and things — *Anne, Cleveland,* and *Metropolitan Stadium* — and they are capitalized. These words are not ordinarily preceded by determiners.

For further discussion of the noun see the following sections in Part 3:

Errors in Subject and Verb Agreement (**agr**), p. 49
Errors in Case Form (**ca**), p. 54

Pronouns

Pronouns are words that replace or refer to nouns. The noun that is referred to is called the *antecedent* of a pronoun.

Cliff drank twelve beers last night. *He* was in no condition to drive home. [*Cliff* is the antecedent of the pronoun *he*.]

Pronouns can be divided into several classes as determined by their form and function.

Personal pronouns take different forms, called *cases,* that are determined by their function in the sentence. Those pronouns (and nouns) that are used as subjects are in the *subjective case,* those that are used as objects are in the *objective case,* and those that show possession are in the *possessive case.* Personal pronouns refer to an individual or a group. The following chart lists the subjective, objective, and possessive case for personal pronouns:

SUBJECTIVE CASE	OBJECTIVE CASE	POSSESSIVE CASE
I	me	my, mine
you	you	you, yours
he, she, it	him, her, it	his, hers, its
we	us	our, ours
they	them	their, theirs

Reflexive pronouns "reflect" or look back to the noun or pronoun acting as the subject. *He* is the subject in the example below.

He cut *himself* with the scissors.

The reflexive pronouns are:

SINGULAR	PLURAL
myself	ourselves
yourself	yourselves
himself	themselves
herself	
itself	

NOTE: "Theirselves" is incorrect.

Intensive pronouns have the same form as reflexive pronouns and they emphasize a noun or pronoun.

The President *himself* went to the meeting.

Relative pronouns — *who, whom, whose, which,* and *that* — join a subordinate or dependent clause to a main or independent clause. An independent clause can stand alone as a sentence; a subordinate or dependent clause cannot stand alone.

The child *who* fell from the balcony broke his arm. [*The child broke his arm* is an independent clause. *Who fell from the balcony* is a dependent clause.]

(See p. 36 for a more detailed discussion of clauses.)

Interrogative pronouns are used to introduce questions. *Who, whom, whose, which,* and *what* are interrogative pronouns.

Who stole the teacher's answer book?

Demonstrative pronouns point to nouns. They may be used as adjectives in the article position just before a noun, as shown in this example:

This dog is gentle.

They may also be used alone as a pronoun, as shown here:

This is the wrong address.

Indefinite pronouns do not substitute for specific nouns. They do, however, function as nouns. *Someone, anyone, each,* and *some* are examples of indefinite pronouns.

Someone will win the race.

For further discussion of the pronoun see the following sections in Part 3:

Errors in Subject and Verb Agreement (**agr**), p. 49

Errors in Case Form (**ca**), p. 54

Errors in the Use of Pronouns: Reference and Agreement (**ref**), p. 142

Faulty Subordination (**sub**), p. 153

Verbs

A verb is an essential part of every sentence and it expresses an action or state of being. A verb reveals what a noun or a pronoun does or what it is.

Verbs are most easily identified by form. They change form to indicate a change of time (*tense*). All tenses except present and past add a word to the verb called an **auxiliary verb**.

PRESENT	PAST	FUTURE
Gerry *walks*	Gerry *walked*	Gerry *will walk*
PRESENT PERFECT	PAST PERFECT	FUTURE PERFECT
Gerry *has walked*	Gerry *had walked*	Gerry *will have walked*

It will be useful for you to remember that all verbs have principal parts: an infinitive form which is preceded by the word *to*, a present participle form which ends in *ing*, a past tense form which ends in *ed* for regular verbs, and a past participle form which ends in *ed* for regular verbs. **Irregular verbs** form the past tense and the past participle differently as in *throw, threw, thrown* and *grow, grew, grown*. All English verbs, then, form principal parts and may be identified by whether or not they can form the following pattern:

INFINITIVE	PRESENT	PAST
to walk	walks	walked
to run	runs	ran

PRESENT PARTICIPLE	PAST PARTICIPLE	
walking	walked	(regular)
running	ran	(irregular)

Transitive verbs are action verbs that require a direct object to complete their meaning. The action is done to someone or something. The **direct object** receives the action of the verb.

Betsy throws baseballs.
Calvin catches baseballs.

In each sentence *baseballs* is the direct object because it is the recipient of the action.

Intransitive verbs express a complete action and can stand alone. They do not need a direct object; however, they are often modified by an adverb. These adverbials should not be confused with direct objects. The adverbials describe *time, place, manner,* or *degree* (*when, where, how,* or *how much*).

Justin works.
Justin works *slowly*. [manner]
Justin works *at night*. [time]
Justin works *in the cafeteria*. [place]

Linking verbs are followed by a *predicate noun* or a *predicate adjective*. The predicate noun tells what the subject is.

George is *a teacher*.
Ronald became *an engineer*.

The predicate adjective describes the subject.

Alexander is *short*.
Emily seems *nervous*.

Linking verbs do not convey an action, and they cannot stand alone. They express a state of being or name one of the senses: *to be, to appear, to remain, to seem, to become, to taste,* and *to feel*. Linking verbs, then, link (or join) the subject to the predicate noun or predicate adjective.

For further discussion of the verb see the following sections in Part 3:

Errors in Subject and Verb Agreement (**agr**), p. 49
Sentence Fragments (**frag**), p. 78
Ineffective Use of the Passive Voice (**pas**), p. 140
Errors in Verb Tense (**t**), p. 156

Adjectives

An adjective modifies a noun. It describes, qualifies, or limits the meaning of the noun with which it is paired.

happy man
original example

Parts of Speech

The position of the adjective is usually before a noun or after a linking verb.

The _____ child.

She seems _____ .

The simplest form of the adjective is called the *positive* form. Adjectives can be changed in form to compare two or more things. When two nouns are compared, the ending *-er* is usually added to the adjective. This is called the *comparative* form of the adjective. When more than two nouns are compared, the ending *-est* is often added to the positive form. This is called the *superlative* form. The following examples show the positive, comparative, and superlative forms of the words *happy* and *strange*.

POSITIVE	COMPARATIVE	SUPERLATIVE
happy	happier	happiest
strange	stranger	strangest

Some adjectives form the comparative and superlative with *more* and *most* rather than with *-er* and *-est*. Usually word length determines whether *more* or *most* is used. Words of three or more syllables generally take *more* and *most* as shown in the examples below; shorter words add *-er* and *-est* as shown in the examples above.

POSITIVE	COMPARATIVE	SUPERLATIVE
original	more original	most original
beautiful	more beautiful	most beautiful

Some adjectives are irregular, and you will need to learn their comparative and superlative forms. The following are examples of irregular adjectives:

POSITIVE	COMPARATIVE	SUPERLATIVE
good	better	best
bad	worse	worst
many	more	most

For further discussion of the adjective see the following sections in Part 3:

Misuse of Adjectives and Adverbs (**ad**), p. 45
Misplaced Modifiers (**mm**), p. 91

Adverbs

Adverbs are also words that describe, qualify, or limit. They modify verbs, adjectives, occasionally other adverbs, and sometimes a whole sentence. Adverbs describe *time, place, manner,* and *degree,* thus telling *when, where, how,* and *how much.*

Frank eats *noisily*. [manner]
Carol ran *upstairs*. [place]
Gregory drank the ale *yesterday*. [time]

Adverbs frequently end in *-ly*. Many adverbs are formed by adding *-ly* to adjectives.

ADJECTIVE	ADVERB
sad	sadly
slow	slowly
anxious	anxiously

There are, however, many adverbs that do not end in *-ly*. Many adverbs that express time or place are of this type.

often   inside
there   here
never

Most adverbs that express the manner of an action do end in *-ly*.

rapidly
humorlessly
happily

Adverbs are not recognized by position as easily as adjectives. Adjectives occupy a fixed position, whereas adverbs can often be moved from one sentence position to another, as the following sentences show.

Frequently Sam goes to the saloon.
Sam goes to the saloon *frequently*.

Sam *frequently* goes to the saloon.

For further discussion of the adverb see the following sections in Part 3:

Misuse of Adjectives and Adverbs (**ad**), p. 45
Misplaced Modifiers (**mm**), p. 91

Prepositions

A preposition connects a noun or a pronoun with other parts of a sentence. A preposition and the noun or pronoun that follow it are needed to form a *prepositional phrase*. In addition, there may be descriptive words in a prepositional phrase. In the following examples the phrase is underlined once and the preposition, twice.

<u>in the drawer</u>
<u>on the table</u>

Prepositions differ from the form words defined earlier (see p. 19). Nouns, verbs, adjectives, and adverbs all have meanings; their meaning often determines their use. Prepositions, on the other hand, have limited meaning. They often suggest position or direction, but they are defined more readily by their functions in relationship to other words in the sentence. (The prepositional phrase which functions as either an adjective or an adverb will be discussed further in the section on phrases in this part (on p. 34).

Dottie raced *into* the bookstore.

In the preceding example, the preposition *into* is best defined as a direction word that connects the verb *raced* with the noun *bookstore*.

Although we use prepositions with great frequency, the entire list of them is short. Some of the most common are:

about	among	below	concerning
above	around	beneath	despite
across	as	beside	down
after	at	between	during
against	before	beyond	except (but)
along	behind	by	excepting

for	off	round	underneath
from	on	since	unlike
in	onto	through	until
inside	out	throughout	up
into	outside	till	upon
like	over	to	with
near	past	toward	within
of	regarding	under	without

Conjunctions

Like prepositions, conjunctions are also words that connect. Conjunctions function to coordinate and to subordinate.

Coordinating conjunctions. Coordinating conjunctions join two constructions — words with words, phrases with phrases, clauses with clauses, and sentences with sentences — that are grammatically equal. There are seven coordinating conjunctions: *and, but, or, for, yet, nor,* and *so.*

It was quite late, *yet* the pizzeria was still open.

Pepperoni *and* cheese are delicious on pizza.

Caroline likes anchovies, *but* David likes mushrooms.

Correlative conjunctions. Correlative conjunctions come in pairs and they join pairs of different constructions that are grammatically equal.

both . . . and
not only . . . but also
either . . . or
neither . . . nor

Gwen asked for *both* anchovies *and* green peppers.

He was *neither* wise *nor* foolish.

Conjunctive adverbs. Conjunctive adverbs are like coordinating conjunctions in that they join two independent clauses, but

Parts of Speech

they call for special punctuation. They must be preceded by a semicolon and followed by a comma. The following list shows some of the words commonly used as conjunctive adverbs:

accordingly	moreover
also	otherwise
besides	nonetheless
consequently	then
furthermore	therefore
however	thus
indeed	

Here are two examples of how conjunctive adverbs are used in sentences:

> He studied frequently; *nevertheless,* he failed the course.
>
> The doctor considered Elvira's condition serious; *however,* he did not consider it life-threatening.

When conjunctive adverbs are used in other sentence positions, they must be surrounded by commas.

> Mary was punished by her mother. Her father, *however,* came to her aid.

For further discussion of coordination see the following sections in Part 3:

> Faulty Coordination (**coord**), p. 65
> Uses of the Comma (**p/,**), p. 102
> Uses of the Semicolon (**p/;**), p. 109

Also see the Sentences section, pp. 31–39, later in this part.

Subordinating conjunctions. Subordinating conjunctions join a word, phrase, or clause to a sentence by making it dependent on the sentence. The idea that is introduced by the subordinating conjunction is not complete by itself. Subordinating conjunctions express different relationships — cause-and-effect, contrast, time, and place, to name a few. The following list shows some of the words frequently used as subordinating conjunctions:

after	because	provided	until
although	before	since	when
as	how	so that	whenever
as if	if	than	where
as long as	in order that	that	wherever
as much as	inasmuch as	though	whether
as though	once	unless	while

Here are two examples of how subordinating conjunctions are used:

After the movie was over, the group of senior citizens went out for pizza. [time]

Oliver left his car at home *because* it is difficult to drive in the city. [cause-and-effect]

Articles

An article is a word that signals that a noun is soon to follow. *The, a,* or *an* are the most common articles.

A glass was cracked.

The glass was cracked.

Other words that can be used in the article position include:

every glass   *several* glasses
this glass   *John's* glass
our glass   *two* glasses
his glass

You will note that many of these words can also be classified as other parts of speech:

our [possessive pronoun]
John's [possessive noun]

Interjections

An interjection is any word or phrase spoken with heavy emphasis or marked with an exclamation point.

Hey!   Ouch!   Look out!

Sentences

EXERCISE

Identify the part of speech of the italicized words in each of the following sentences.

1. May the *better* person win.
2. Pull *up* the shades, and *the* room will be *brighter*.
3. Jerry's *suggestion* is nonsense.
4. An expert in *economics* is scheduled to speak *next*.
5. The *tomato* plants in our garden are dying for lack *of water*.
6. The salesman spoke *neither* English *nor* Spanish.
7. *Only* a *few* of the shows are *produced* for children.
8. Coffee *smells delightful* to *many* people.
9. The building contains *three* miles of *hallways*.
10. Grapefruit *without* sugar is *too sour*.
11. *Maria's wool* suit was beginning to make her itch.
12. *Even* Matt argued that the decision was *hasty* and *unfair*.
13. The first ten rows of seats will *probably* be reserved.
14. Caroline collected maps from *every* state *but* Alaska.
15. A tunnel runs *under* the *river*.
16. Sponsors *often* complain *about* censorship.
17. Nine o'clock was *too late for supper*.
18. *There* is a course in astronomy given at the university.
19. *Walking* can be a welcome relief *to* driving.
20. Arthur *snatched* a cookie *from* the table and ran *outside*.

SENTENCES

All of the parts of speech discussed in the preceding section represent the individual words that combine to form sentences. To write clear sentences, it is essential that you understand how the parts of speech combine with each other. All sentences can be divided into a subject and a predicate. That is to say that all sentences accomplish two things: (1) they name something (subject), and (2) they make a statement about what has been named (predicate).

SUBJECT   PREDICATE
Dogs   bite.
Abused dogs   may bite unsuspecting strangers.

It is difficult to punctuate a sentence properly if you cannot identify the complete subject and the complete predicate.

Subjects

The subject of a sentence is what you make a statement about. The predicate is what you say about the subject. The subject is a noun, pronoun, or word cluster that functions as a noun (*nominal*). The simplest subject is a noun or pronoun. The simple subject is often the headword of a cluster of words that functions as a noun. A headword, combined with all of its modifiers, is called a *noun phrase*, and this is the complete subject. In each of the following examples, the complete subject is underlined once and the simple subject is underlined twice. (A useful way to find the subject of most sentences is to ask who or what about the verb.)

The river forms the boundary. [What forms the boundary?]
The man in the gray suit looks unhappy. [Who looks unhappy?]

In English, most sentences are formed with the subject preceding the verb. These sentences make a statement and are called **declarative sentences**. Some sentences, however, begin with *there* or *it*. These words serve to delay the subject until after the verb. *There* and *it* are called *expletives*. A simple subject is underlined in the first and second examples below, and a group of words that function as a noun (*noun clause*) is underlined as the subject of the third.

Fourteen goldfish are in the bowl.
There are fourteen goldfish in the bowl.
It is unfortunate that Shirley dropped her tray.

Questions (**interrogative sentences**) frequently invert the positions of the subject and the verb.

Are *you* going to class?
Did *you* eat the spaghetti?

Is *Eric* going to the rock concert?

The subject is omitted or understood in commands (**imperative sentences**).

Turn left at the next light. [*You* is the understood subject.]
Watch the telephone pole. [*You* is the understood subject.]

Predicates

The predicate is the part of the sentence that asserts or tells something about the subject. Every predicate contains at least one verb. Most predicates, however, consist of the verb (which is the headword) that shows tense, its complements (if there are any), and all modifiers. A **complement** is a word or construction that completes the meaning of the verb.

The youthful rioters broke every window in the office building. [The headword is the simple verb *broke* which is followed by the complement, *every window,* and modifier, *in the office building.*]

Complements

Many predicates consist of a verb and its complements. The four most important types of complements are *direct object, indirect object, subject complement* (predicate noun and adjective), and *object complement*.

Direct object.   A direct object is the person or thing that receives the action of the transitive verb. A direct object answers the question what or whom about the verb.

The delivery man lost his *truck.* [What did the man lose?]
Connie left her *friends.* [Whom did Connie leave?]

Indirect object.   An indirect object usually occurs with and precedes a direct object. It tells to whom or for whom the action of a verb is directed.

Rod bought his *puppy* a collar.
Jackie sent his *minister* a message.

The indirect object can always be made into the object of the preposition *to* or *for* and placed after the direct object.

> Rod bought a collar *for his puppy*.
> Jackie sent a message *to his minister*.

Subject complement. Subject complements are often called *predicate nouns* and *predicate adjectives*. A subject complement can only follow a linking verb. It is not to be confused with a direct object which can only follow a transitive verb. (See the section about verbs, p. 23.)

A predicate noun follows a linking verb and further explains or renames the subject.

> Bernard is a *mathematician*.
> Debby became *president* of her class.

A predicate adjective is an adjective that follows a linking verb and describes the subject.

> The sun seems *warm* and *soothing*.
> The veterinarian is *angry*.

Object complement. An object complement follows a direct object and explains it further. Object complements can be both nouns and adjectives.

> The committee appointed Emily *chairperson*. [noun]
> The appointment made Emily *happy*. [adjective]

Phrases

A phrase is a group of related words that function as a grammatical unit. Unlike a clause, a phrase does not have a subject and a predicate. You should be able to recognize *prepositional phrases, verbal phrases, verb phrases, noun phrases,* and *absolute phrases*.

Prepositional phrases. A prepositional phrase consists of a preposition followed by its object — a noun or a pronoun — and any words that modify the noun or pronoun. Prepositional phrases usually function as adjectives and adverbs.

The man *with the eye patch* is a pirate. [adjective]
The puppy is hiding *under the bed*. [place adverb]

Verbal phrases. Writers must be careful not to confuse verbs and verbals. *Verbals* are verb forms that cannot function as sentence verbs; rather, they function as nouns, adjectives, and adverbs. These forms include gerunds (*-ing* ending), present participles (*-ing* ending), past participles (usually *-ed* ending), and infinitives (*to* before verb).

A *verbal phrase* is a verbal with its objects and modifiers. The verbal is generally the first word of the phrase. The three types of verbal phrases are *participial phrases, gerund phrases,* and *infinitive phrases.*

Participial phrases. Participial phrases consist of a present or past participle followed by its modifiers. Participial phrases function as adjectives. Present participles have an *-ing* ending, and past participles usually have *-ed* endings.

Walking briskly, the doctor entered the emergency room. [The present participial phrase modifies *doctor.*]
The car *parked near the stadium* is in front of a fire hydrant. [The past participial phrase modifies *car.*]

Gerund phrases. A gerund is the *-ing* form of a verb that functions as a noun. A gerund phrase consists of a gerund plus its object and modifiers.

Fishing in the river is his idea of fun. [The gerund phrase is the subject of the sentence.]

Infinitive phrases. An infinitive is the form of the verb that can be preceded naturally by *to* — *to walk, to read.* An infinitive phrase consists of an infinitive and all of its modifiers. The infinitive phrase may function as a noun, an adjective, or an adverb.

Roger likes *to eat lobster.* [noun]
The person *to lead us* must be intelligent. [adjective]
The conductor ran *to catch his train.* [adverb]

Verb phrases. A verb phrase is not to be confused with a verbal phrase. Auxiliary verbs such as *shall, will, have, has, had, do, does, did,* and forms of *be,* are used with main verbs to indicate tense and emphasis. Combinations of the auxiliaries and the main verb are called verb phrases.

> I *will be going* soon.
>
> John *has gone* already.

Auxiliaries such as *can, could, may, shall* and *will* are called *modals* (helping verbs) and combine with the main verb to indicate such qualities as necessity, obligation, and permission. The two kinds of auxiliaries can work together to form more complex verb phrases.

> I *may have been going.*

Noun phrases. A noun phrase consists of a main noun, or headword, and a combination of determiners and modifiers. You will need to isolate the headword of a noun phrase, that is, the simple subject of the sentence, in order to understand subject and verb agreement.

> *A load of books* is in *the wagon.* [Note that the singular verb agrees in number with the headword *load,* also singular, and not the plural *books* which is the object of a preposition.]

Absolute phrases. Absolute phrases modify whole sentences rather than individual words or word groups. In this sense they are *absolutely* alone. Absolute phrases usually consist of at least a participle and its subject. They are not grammatically related to the rest of the sentence by a conjunction.

> *The storm having subsided,* the sailors cast off.

Clauses

A clause is a group of words that has a subject and a predicate. If the clause is complete by itself and makes sense, it is called *independent.* A clause that cannot stand alone is called *dependent.*

Sentences

Independent clauses. If a group of words with a subject and predicate can stand alone and make sense, that group is an independent clause. In effect, an independent clause is a simple sentence.

Arthur insulted the fat lady in the bakery.

See the section on sentence types on p. 38 for a discussion of the relationship of independent and dependent clauses.

Dependent clauses. Although dependent clauses also have a subject and a predicate, they do not make sense alone because they literally depend on an independent clause to complete their meaning. Dependent clauses can be recognized by the subordinating words that join them to the independent clause — *although, after, as, as if, since, who, which, when, before,* to name a few. Dependent clauses function as a grammatical unit by acting as nouns, adjectives, and adverbs.

Dependent clause as a noun clause. Noun clauses function as nouns in a sentence. They usually function as subjects or direct objects.

That Jenny moved out of town does not surprise me. [subject]

NOTE: Notice the structure of the dependent clause in the example above: subordinator (*that*) + subject (*Jenny*) + verb (*moved*).

Fred always buys *what his friends tell him.* [direct object]

NOTE: Notice the structure of the dependent clause in the example above: relative pronoun (*what*) + subject (*his friends*) + verb (*tell*).

Dependent clause as an adjective clause. Adjective clauses modify a noun or a pronoun. They generally begin with a relative pronoun such as *who, whom, which,* and *that.* They usually follow the noun that they modify.

The man *who left his hat* is absentminded.

The jogger remembers the dog *that bit his ankle.*

Dependent clause as an adverb clause. Adverb clauses modify verbs, adjectives, and other adverbs. They may occur in various sentence positions, and they are usually introduced by subordinating conjunctions.

Because Theresa was ill, Frank made the speech.
Many people have moved *since the river flooded the town.*

Sentence types

Sentence types are determined by varying combinations of clauses. There are four sentence types: *simple, compound, complex,* and *compound-complex.*

Simple sentence. Simple sentences have one subject and one verb. The simple sentence contains one independent clause and no dependent clauses.

The <u>visitors</u> <u>will leave</u> on Thursday. [a simple subject, *visitors,* and a simple verb, *will leave*]

<u>Patsy and Bill</u> <u>enjoy</u> windsurfing. [a compound subject, *Patsy and Bill,* and a single verb, *enjoy*]

<u>Winston</u> <u>drank and smoked</u> all night. [a simple subject, *Winston,* and a compound verb, *drank and smoked*]

Compound sentence. Compound sentences consist of two or more independent clauses joined by a comma and a coordinating conjunction, a semicolon, or a conjunctive adverb.

Yesterday Guy went to the theater [independent] and *Carol went shopping* [independent].

The auditorium was nearly empty [independent]; nevertheless, *the cast went on with the play* [independent].

Cars should be parked to the left [independent]; *trucks to the right* [independent]. [The verb *should be parked* is understood in the second independent clause.]

Complex sentence. Complex sentences combine one independent clause with one or more dependent clauses.

The Yankees won the playoffs [independent] *because they had stronger relief pitching* [dependent].

Exercise 39

Compound-complex sentence. Compound-complex sentences consist of two or more independent clauses and at least one dependent clause.

Even though the storm subsided [dependent], *the game was postponed* [independent], and *the spectators were issued tickets for a later date* [independent].

EXERCISE

Identify all of the complement(s) in each of the following sentences as direct object, indirect object, subject complement, or object complement.
1. The student body elected Bruce president.
2. Lucy gave her father a bottle of cologne.
3. The patient seems better.
4. Phil entered the Boston Marathon.
5. Catherine is secretary and treasurer.

Identify the types of phrases that are italicized in each of the following sentences as either prepositional, verbal, verb, noun, or absolute phrases.
1. *Parking in this lot* is illegal.
2. Jeff likes *to read German literature.*
3. *The rain having stopped,* the children went to the playground.
4. *Playing in Fenway Park* is his son's only wish.
5. The teacher *may have been smoking* in the classroom.

Underline the dependent clauses in the following sentences and identify their function (noun, adjective, or adverb).
1. That the car has air-conditioning is an important consideration.
2. The minister who always stuttered is seeing a speech therapist.
3. Until Susan stepped out of the car, Julie did not recognize her own sister.
4. Nancy left the prom early because she was ill.
5. I realize that he is a good soldier.

Identify the sentence type of each of the following (simple, compound, complex, or compound-complex).
1. Terry dropped the cup, and the handle broke off.
2. Professor Whitty left, but he returned a few minutes later.
3. The witness whom he talked to was not the one who saw the accident.
4. The first question was easy, but the second one was difficult.
5. David changed the oil before he left, and Peggy checked the tires later.

3
An Alphabetical List of Frequent Writing Problems

1
ABBREVIATIONS `ab`

Abbreviations save writers time and space, and so they are used extensively in technical reports, addresses, formal lists, and informal correspondence. Only a few, however, are acceptable in the writing done for English composition courses. When in doubt about whether to use an abbreviation, do not use it — spell out the word(s). (A discussion of the use of abbreviations in footnote and bibliography forms appears in Part 4.)

Titles

The following abbreviations are acceptable in most contexts.
Abbreviate titles before and after proper names and degrees and special awards after proper names.

Before	After
Mr. Michael Kelly	Maria Lopez, A.B.
Mrs. Robin Grant	Mark Weston, B.A.
Ms. Andrea Kline	David Gilmour, M.D.
Hon. Mary Pender	Jeanette Lacrosse, Ph.D.
Dr. David Gilmour	Christine Newhart, D.D.S.

BEFORE | AFTER
Sen. Mark Hatfield | Oscar Golding, D.V.M.
Rev. Theresa Jordan | Henry Frazier, Esq.
Col. Henry Schultz | Larry Gress, M.A.

NOTE: Titles and degrees after proper names are preceded by a comma.

Technical terms

Abbreviate frequently used and easily recognized technical terms.

cc (cubic centimeter)
cm (centimeter)
km (kilometer)
kmh (kilometers per hour)
mpg (miles per gallon)
mph (miles per hour)
rpm (revolutions per minute)

Time

Abbreviate expressions of time.

B.C.
A.D.
A.M.
P.M.
EST (eastern standard time)
DST (daylight saving time)

Familiar names

Use familiar abbreviations for the names of organizations, government agencies, institutions, and some people and countries.

NAACP, CORE, AAUP, YMCA
IBM, NBC, ITT
FDR, LBJ, JFK
USA, USSR

Write out something less familiar with the abbreviation following in parentheses the first time that it is used. Subsequent uses may employ the abbreviation:

Public Service of New Hampshire (PSNH)

Foreign phrases

Abbreviate standard foreign phrases. Reserve foreign phrases for formal writing, footnotes, and bibliographies. In less formal writing it is customary to use the English word or phrase.

e.g. (for example)
etc. (and so forth)
c (circa — about)
N.B. (note well)
cf (compare with)
et al. (and others)

Currency and percentages

Abbreviate dollars and cents and percentages.

$8.59
53.5%

The examples above present representative abbreviations. Other abbreviations of the same types are acceptable. You will find these in your desk dictionary.

The following abbreviations are not acceptable in formal writing.

Other titles

Do not abbreviate titles (except as specified above) and first names.

President [not Pres.]
Professor [not Prof.]
Representative [not Rep.]
George [not Geo.]

Units of measure
Do not abbreviate units of measurement.

ounce [not oz.]
pounds [not lbs.]
feet [not ft.]

Geographical names
Do not abbreviate geographical names.

New York [not N. Y.]
street [not st.]

Days, months, and holidays
Do not abbreviate days, months, and holidays.

Friday [not Fri.]
August [not Aug.]
Christmas [not Xmas]

School courses
Do not abbreviate courses of instruction.

economics [not econ.]
sociology [not soc.]

Common words
Do not abbreviate common words.

year [not yr.]
building [not bldg.]

Elements of official names
Do not use Inc., Co., and the ampersand (&) unless they are part of an official name.

(See Uses of the Period, p. 99 for a discussion of punctuating abbreviations.)

EXERCISE

Correct any of the following sentences that contain faulty abbreviations. Use C to designate a correct sentence.

1. Our biology prof. was born on Dec. 13, 1941 in Columbus, O.
2. Address any questions to Noel Cartwright, Ph.D.
3. Sen. Burant claimed that his new Trans Am got twenty mpg on a trip to Houston.
4. Geo. Washington's Birthday is no longer celebrated on Feb. 22.
5. The package that UPS delivered weighed seven lbs. and nine ounces.

2
MISUSE OF ADJECTIVES AND ADVERBS ad

Adjectives and adverbs modify other words in a sentence, and each has a distinct function. Adjectives modify nouns and pronouns; adverbs modify verbs, adjectives, and other adverbs. Ordinarily, each has a distinct form. Adverbs usually end in *-ly*, and they are often formed by adding *-ly* to adjectives: *brisk, briskly; different, differently.*

Henry's grandfather took a *brisk* walk after the Thanksgiving feast. [adjective modifying noun *walk*]

Henry's grandfather walked *briskly* after the Thanksgiving feast. [adverb modifying verb *walked*]

Adjectives are generally recognized by their position in a sentence. They usually appear before the noun that they modify:

He ran into a *brick* wall.

Adjectives also appear after a linking verb to describe the subject:

The employees were *excited*.

Adverbs frequently follow the verb that they modify, but usually precede the adjective or other adverb that they modify. Most adverbs tell *where, when,* or *how* an action took place. These are adverbs of *place, time, manner,* or *degree* and most adverbs are one of these types.

PLACE — WHERE? TIME — WHEN?
there   always
downtown   never
outside   soon

MANNER — HOW?   DEGREE — HOW MUCH?
carefully   very
silently   quite
quietly   somewhat
                 always

The misuse of adjectives and adverbs occurs most frequently in one of the following situations.

Linking verbs and modifiers

Use adjectives after linking verbs. Use adverbs when the modifier describes a verb. Adjectives are used after verbs such as *be, become, appear, seem, look, feel, sound, smell,* and *taste.* (Note that these verbs are "sense" verbs or verbs like *to be* that need an adjective to describe their state.) These verbs are called *linking verbs,* and they are correctly followed by an adjective. When a modifier describes a verb, the adverb is used. Note that *well* is an adverb but it is used as an adjective when referring to health.

Pam looked *eager* before the guests arrived. [adjective]
Pam looked *eagerly* for her missing gerbil. [adverb]
Amy is *good.* [adjective referring to behavior]
Amy is *well.* [adverb referring to health — used as an adjective following a linking verb, see p. 48]

Comparisons

Use the correct forms of regular adjectives and adverbs to make comparisons. The comparative and superlative degrees of adjectives and adverbs are formed by adding *-er* or *-est.* Longer adjectives of three or more syllables and adverbs of two or more syllables are compared with *more* and *most.* Occasionally both methods are acceptable. In such cases *more* and *most* make the comparison more emphatic.

The snake was slim*er* than the frog. [less emphatic and less desirable]

The snake was *more* slimy than the frog. [more emphatic comparison and more desirable]

But avoid using both methods:

The snake was *more slimier* than the frog. [incorrect]

Use *less* and *least* for all reversed or negative comparisons. The following examples summarize the rules just presented for comparisons.

	POSITIVE	COMPARATIVE	SUPERLATIVE
Adjectives	clean	cleaner	cleanest
	genuine	more/less genuine	most/least genuine
Adverbs	fast	faster	fastest
	swiftly	more/less swiftly	most/least swiftly

Remember these rules when making comparisons:

1. The comparative compares one thing with one other.

   a *thicker* sandwich [than that one]

   a *more attractive* wardrobe [than that one]

2. The superlative form compares one thing with two or more things.

   the *thickest* sandwich [of all]

   the *most attractive* wardrobe [of all]

   Jake's friend is the *youngest* of six children. [*Youngest* rather than *younger* is correct because more than two children are being compared.]

Irregular forms

Use the correct form of irregular adjectives and adverbs. Irregular adjectives and adverbs are not compared with *-er* and *-est* and *more* and *most*. The following words are the comparative forms of some irregular adjectives and adverbs.

ad | 48 An Alphabetical List of Frequent Writing Problems

	POSITIVE	COMPARATIVE	SUPERLATIVE
Adjectives	good	better	best
	bad	worse	worst
	some	more	most
Adverbs	well	better	best
	badly	worse	worst

The following pairs of words often cause problems for writers who incorrectly use them interchangeably.

ADJECTIVES	ADVERBS
real	really
good	well
sure	surely

Bonnie was a *real good* student. [incorrect]
Bonnie was a *really good* student. [correct]

Well is used as an adjective in reference to health only. Otherwise, it is an adverb.

Patricia looks *good*. [predicate adjective meaning attractive]
Patricia looks *well*. [adjective meaning healthy]
She performed her tasks *well*. [adverb of manner]

EXERCISE

Correct the following sentences for misuse of adjectives and adverbs. Draw an arrow from the adjectives and adverbs to the words that they modify. Use C to designate a correct sentence.

1. The high jumper cleared the bar easy.
2. The fishing trip to Greenland was one of the more pleasant experiences he ever had.
3. It sure can't be disputed that Reggie Jackson is a powerful hitter.
4. Becky was real shocked when her turtle died.
5. The robin's song sounds clear.
6. The spaghetti smells badly.
7. Amy felt badly about fighting with her sister.
8. Paul Newman is the best of the two actors.

9. Johnson, Murray, and Partridge were all wise men, but Murray was the wiser.
10. The students could not determine which one of the three teachers was better.
11. "How are you today?" "Good, thank you."

3
ERRORS IN SUBJECT AND VERB AGREEMENT `agr`

(NOTE: Errors in pronoun and antecedent agreement are discussed in Errors in the Use of Pronouns: Reference and Agreement, p. 142.)

A verb must agree with its subject in person and number. (Singular subjects take singular verbs, and subjects in the third person take verbs in the third person.) Since most English verbs conjugate regularly, this problem is limited. Here is the present tense conjugation of the regular English verb *to study*.

	SINGULAR	PLURAL
First person	I study	we study
Second person	you study	you study
Third person	he stud*ies*	they study

Only one of the six forms is different — third person singular. It is not surprising, then, that most confusion with subject and verb agreement relates to this one form. The past tense is not a problem because all of the forms are the same as shown in the example below. An exception to this is the verb *to be*. It has two past forms: *was* is singular and *were* is plural.

	SINGULAR	PLURAL
First person	I studied	we studied
Second person	you studied	you studied
Third person	he studied	they studied

The other tenses are formed with auxiliary verbs (*to be* and *to have*) and will be discussed below. (See Part 2, pp. 23–24, for a more complete discussion of verb forms.)

In the present tense the singular subject has no -s ending, but the singular third person verb does (*I throw, he throws*). Writers tend to associate the -*s* ending with the plural of nouns which, of course, is correct. Confusion often results when this association transfers to verb forms.

> The student studies in the library. [singular subject and -*s* ending on singular verb]

Conversely, in the plural the subject has an -*s* ending while the verb does not.

> The students study in the library. [-*s* ending on plural subject]

Perhaps most of the confusion with this -*s* ending of the third person singular involves the irregular verbs *to be, to do,* and *to have.* In each, the third person singular ends in -*s*, and to this extent, the verbs are regular.

> I am   I do   I have
> you are   you do   you have
> he i*s*   he doe*s*   he ha*s*

The plural forms of these verbs are the more regular — *are, do,* and *have,* respectively.

Making subjects and verbs agree is not usually a problem with short sentences. Many writers, however, have difficulty with larger constructions in which there may be more than one subject, or in which the subject is a noun phrase. If the subject is a noun phrase, the verb must agree with the headword or simple subject.

> A mangy *dog* with three puppies lives at the town dump. [The headword, *dog,* is singular and it agrees with the singular verb form, *lives.*]

Errors in subject and verb agreement occur most frequently in the constructions described below.

Compound subjects

Subjects joined by *and* agree with plural verbs.

> Mary and the children *were* on the roller coaster.
> Becky and Cathy *are* in the chorus.

EXCEPTION: When the two or more elements of the compound subject form a single unit or refer to a singular verb.

3 / Errors in Subject and Verb Agreement   51   agr

Bacon and eggs *is* my favorite breakfast.
Twenty dollars *is* a reasonable offer.

When compound subjects are joined with *or, nor, either . . . or,* or *neither . . . nor* the verb must agree with the noun that is closer.

Either the students or the teacher *has* bolted the door. [singular]
Either the teacher or the students *have* bolted the door. [plural]
Neither Ted nor Alice *was* acquainted with Bob. [singular]
Neither the dogs nor the cats *stay* in the yard. [plural]

Indefinite pronouns

Among the indefinite pronouns that are always singular and therefore require a singular verb are *each, one, another, anything, no one, everyone, someone, something, either, everybody, somebody,* and *nobody*.

Either of the candidates *is* acceptable. [The verb does not agree with the word *candidates* because it is not the subject. *Candidates* is the object of a prepositional phrase modifying the subject, *either*.]
Somebody *left* the camera at Oliver's house.

Among the indefinite pronouns that are clearly plural and require a plural verb are *both, many,* and *several.*

Both of the students *are* attending the assembly.

Indefinite pronouns that express quantity — *more, all, any, none,* and *some* — may take either singular or plural verbs. Agreement is determined by the meaning of the noun or of the pronoun that follows. This rule also applies to fractions and percentages.

All of the *campers are* in the shelter. [plural]
All of the *money is* lost. [singular]
A third of the *students have* passed the test. [plural]
Seventy-five percent of his *allowance is* spent on food. [singular]

Collective nouns

A collective noun refers to a group and agrees with either a singular or plural verb. This agreement is based on a logical rather than a grammatical choice that is determined by the meaning of the sentence. *Class, jury, committee, crowd, team,* and *group* are examples of collective nouns.

> The crowd *is* gathering in front of the stadium. [*Crowd* is acting as a single unit.]
> The jury *have* voted according to their consciences. [*Jury* acts independently unless there is unanimity.]

The collective noun *number* is singular when preceded by *the* and plural when preceded by *a*.

> *The* number of fish in his aquarium is excessive. [singular]
> *A* number of spectators *have left* the game early. [plural]

Nouns plural in form only

Some nouns are plural in form — *physics, athletics, news, politics,* and *economics* — but singular in meaning and require a singular verb.

> Economics *is* a major course of study at most universities.

Inverted word order

Sentences with inverted word order usually begin with the introductory expletive *there* or *here* with the subject that determines the form following the verb.

> There are shade *trees* in the park.
> There is a lonely shade *tree* in the park.

Nouns and pronouns between the subject and verb

Intervening clauses and phrases do not affect the number of the verb.

> The wheel, *as well as the seat and pedals,* was stolen from Becky's unicycle.
> The president *with his advisors* is promoting the new budget.
> Paul, *not his sisters,* plays tennis.

Linking verbs

A linking verb agrees with the subject, not the complement.

Emma's *source* of income *is* interest and insurance.
Interest and insurance are Emma's source of income.

Titles

A title is always singular and requires a singular verb form even when plural nouns are within the title.

The Grapes of Wrath is John Steinbeck's most famous novel.

Nouns of time, money, weight, and measurement

Nouns of time, money, weight, and measurement appear to be plural, but they take a singular verb form.

Eighty dollars *is* exactly what he paid for it.
Four months *is* a long time to be away from home.
One hundred and fifty pounds *is* an unusually light weight for a professional athlete.
Thirty miles *is* a long commute.

Relative pronouns as subjects

When a relative pronoun is the subject, the verb agrees with the noun that is the antecedent of the relative pronoun.

Fred should listen to people who *offer* advice. [verb agrees with *people*]
I have a friend who *lives* in Alaska. [verb agrees with *friend*]
Miki, who gives flute lessons, *works* for a printer. [verb agrees with *Miki*]

EXERCISE

Correct the following sentences for errors in subject and verb agreement. Use C to designate a correct sentence.

1. Every day a group of dogs gather in my garden.
2. Either the turtle or the guppies is to be removed from the small tank.
3. Neither the child nor his parents enjoys magic shows.

4. Each of the contracts appeal to the union leadership.
5. Each of the politicians do not care about incentive programs.
6. None of the actors has been nominated for an award this year.
7. At the beginning of the session there are roll call and inspection.
8. Either a dog and two cats or a mynah bird is in the pet store window.
9. He is one of the students who leaves early.
10. The jury has retired to their hotel rooms for the night.

4
ERRORS IN CASE FORM   ca

Case is the grammatical form of a noun or pronoun that shows the functions of the noun or pronoun in a sentence. There are three different cases in English: the *subjective* (nominative), the *possessive,* and the *objective.* These three cases change the form of personal pronouns, as you can see in the following chart:

	SUBJECTIVE	OBJECTIVE	POSSESSIVE
First person	I, we	me, us	my, mine, our, ours,
Second person	you	you	your, yours
Third person	he, she, it, they	him, her, it, them	his, her, hers, its, their, theirs

The cases also change the form of *who* and *whom.*

SUBJECTIVE	OBJECTIVE	POSSESSIVE
who	whom	whose
whoever	whomever	

Subjective case forms

The subjective case forms are used when the noun or pronoun is used for the subject of a sentence or a clause. It is also the form for predicate nouns.

4 / Errors in Case Form

SUBJECT OF SENTENCE
She and *I* went to the record shop three times.
Maria and *he* vacationed in South Dakota.

SUBJECT OF SUBORDINATE CLAUSE
Give the scholarship to the student *who* has the best academic record.

SUBJECT OF UNDERSTOOD VERB
Alice is taller than *she* (is).

PREDICATE PRONOUNS (after *to be* and other linking verbs)
The slowest runners were *she* and *I*.
The teacher felt that it was *she* who placed a firecracker in his top desk drawer.

Objective case forms

The objective case forms are used when the pronoun is an object. Some possible object positions are the direct or indirect object of a verb or verbal, the object of a preposition, and the subject or object of an infinitive.

DIRECT OBJECT OF A VERB
The members elected *her* chairperson.

OBJECT OF A PREPOSITION
One of *us* will have to leave soon.

OBJECT OF A VERBAL
Convincing *him* was not a simple task.

SUBJECT OF AN INFINITIVE
The class asked *him* to represent them.

Possessive case forms

The possessive case forms are used as adjectives before nouns and gerunds. *My* is used before nouns and *mine* is used as a predicate adjective following a linking verb.

BEFORE NOUNS
His books were under *her* desk.

BEFORE GERUNDS
Her running the marathon was my idea.

MY AND MINE
My sandwich is in the cooler.
The sandwich in the cooler is *mine*.

Note: The possessive form of nouns is discussed in Uses of the Apostrophe, p. 121.

The misuse of case form occurs most frequently in the situations described below.

Compound constructions

A compound construction is one in which two or more elements are coordinated. Always use the subjective case in a compound subject and the objective case in a compound object.

Jackie and I went to the library last night. [subject]
Her two favorite companions were *Larry and he*. [predicate noun. Normally this sentence would be worded *Larry and he were her two favorite companions*.]
The officer gave the warnings to *Alice and him*. [object of preposition]

Writers rarely make a mistake when a single pronoun is a subject or object. For example, it is unlikely that a speaker of English would say:

Him went to the lecture.

However, we frequently hear such mistakes as:

Jeff and *him* went to the lecture.
Arthur and *me* had a driving lesson.

A simple check for correctness is to drop one part of the compound structure. Drop *Jeff* in the above example, and you are left with "Him went to the lecture," which your ear tells you is wrong.

We and us constructions

The case form of the first person plural construction depends on the use of the noun that it precedes.

4 / Errors in Case Form   ca

> All of *us* children lived together. [Children is the object of *of*.]
>
> *We* children grew up together. [Children is the subject of the sentence.]

Perhaps the simplest way to check for accuracy is to drop the noun and then use the pronoun that sounds best.

> All of *we* lived together. [incorrect]
>
> All of *us* lived together. [correct]

Appositives

An appositive renames a noun, and it usually follows that noun. The pronoun should be in agreement with the noun it is in apposition with.

> The voters of the district elected two representatives, *Harold and me*. [*Representatives* is the object of the verb.]
>
> Two representatives, *Harold and I*, were elected by the voters of the district. [*Representatives* is the subject of the clause.]

Than or as

The case of a pronoun after *than* or *as* in an elliptical (incomplete) clause should be the same as if the clause were completed. The pronoun is in the subjective case if it would be the subject of the omitted verb.

> None of the other skiers was as versatile as she [was].

Notice the difference in the following two sentences:

> Pablo admired Robert more than *I* [admired Robert]. [The pronoun is in the subjective case if it would be the subject of the omitted verb.]
>
> Pablo admired Robert more than [he admired] *me*. [The pronoun is in the objective case if it would be the object of the omitted verb.]

Who and whom

The form of the pronoun *who* is determined by its function in its clause. Use *who* (or *whoever*) in subject positions and *whom* (or *whomever*) in object positions. In questions use *who* if the question is about a subject, *whom* if it is about an object.

> *Who* left the groceries in the car? *He* left the groceries in the car. [question about a subject]
>
> *Whom* do you blame? I blame *him*. [question about an object]

Remember that in subordinate clauses the form of *who* is determined by its role in the clause; it is not determined by the function of the clause. A clause may function as a subject, an object, or a modifier.

> Leave the key with *whoever* arrives last. [*Whoever* is the subject of the clause *whoever arrives last*. The clause, however, is the object of the preposition *with*.]
>
> Leave the key with whomever you can trust. [*Whomever* is the object of the verb *can trust*.]

For further discussion of case see pp. 21, 31–34 in Part 2.

EXERCISE

Correct the following sentences for errors in case form. Use C to designate a correct sentence. Be ready to explain the rule that applies to each problem.

1. The principal did not pay any attention to my father and I.
2. My parents worry about me working while I am attending the university.
3. The victim quickly identified the culprits, Vera and she.
4. Whom did you say was at the door?
5. No one on their team is as tall as him.
6. Who is Elaine living with?
7. Thomas Pynchon is interesting because few writers are as original as him.
8. Between she and I, we just finished patching the roof.
9. His two favorite companions were Larry and him.
10. After talking with the teacher, us students went to the principal.

5
CAPITALIZATION AND LOWER CASE FORM `cap/c`

Appropriate capitalization is a matter of convention. This section will list the basic conventions. The rules vary, however, and you should consult a dictionary for specific problems. Many of the conventions are so familiar to us that they need not be illustrated below. Capitalizing the first word of a sentence, the pronoun *I*, and the first letter in the first word of a quotation are among these familiar conventions.

Some capitalization, however, is a matter of style rather than convention. When capitalizing for stylistic purposes, writers usually do so to emphasize a key word. Stylistic capitalization is acceptable and often effective if it is not abused.

Problems in capitalization occur most frequently in the situations described below.

Titles

Capitalize the first word and all important words of titles of books, periodicals, articles, and reports. Also capitalize chapter titles and major divisions. Articles (*a, an, the*) and prepositions of less than five letters and coordinating conjunctions should not be capitalized unless they are the first or last word in a title or subtitle.

The Fellowship of the Ring
"Chapter Four: The Research Paper"
Refections in a Golden Eye

Proper nouns and proper adjectives

Capitalize all proper nouns and adjectives formed from proper nouns.

COMMON NOUN	PROPER NOUN	PROPER ADJECTIVE
nation	France	Frenchman
poet	Wordsworth	Wordsworthian

Capitalize names of specific persons, places, and things.

Edward Kennedy
Portland, Maine

the Empire State Building
Grand Canyon
Mississippi River
Venus [Do not capitalize *earth* unless it is used as a celestial body.]

Capitalize historical events, periods, and documents.

Spanish-American War
the Renaissance
Declaration of Independence

Capitalize days of the week, months, and holidays.

Friday
April
Thanksgiving

Capitalize names of organizations, departments, political, and social groups.

United Way
Department of State
Democrats
Kiwanis
Little League

Capitalize races, nationalities, and languages.

Asian
Germans
French

EXCEPTION: When referring to people, the capitalization of *blacks* or *whites* is optional.

Capitalize religious names for sacred persons and things.

Allah
Buddha
the Bible [but *biblical*]

God
Judaism
Moslem

Honorary and official titles
Capitalize titles only when they precede the name of a person.

Bishop Parker
Prince Andrew
Professor Ferland

Specific school courses
Do not capitalize the name of a general subject or discipline:

chemistry
math

Sam did well in chemistry and math, and he failed Latin.

Do capitalize specific course titles and course titles that are names of languages.

History 412
French
Romantic Poetry
English
Biology I

Arthur's favorite courses were Romantic Poetry and History 412.

Relations
A word that designates a family relationship (*mother, uncle, grandfather*) is capitalized when used with the person's name or as a substitute for the name.

I remember Grandmother Howell's studio.
I remember Aunt Harriet's studio.
The gift was from my Uncle Larry.

Do not capitalize words that show family relationship when used with a possessive pronoun.

I remember *my* grandmother's studio.
The gift was from *his* uncle.

Trade names

Capitalize trade names but not the specific name of the product.

Schlitz beer
Ford car

Abbreviations

Capitalize abbreviations when the whole word or each word in the phrase should be capitalized. Otherwise, the abbreviation should not be capitalized.

the NAACP
the U.S. Post Office
30 mpg
etc.

Directions

Capitalize compass directions only when they name specific regions.

west   the West
south   the South

Pat and Fred drove *west* for two miles before they remembered that they had left their lights on.
Drew and Bonnie spent two weeks travelling in *the West*.

Exceptions

Do not capitalize seasons, academic years, or class designations.

fall semester
junior year

spring
sophomore
winter quarter

Do not capitalize the names of centuries unless a century is used as a specific historical era.

My grandmother lived some of her life in the *nineteenth century.*
Many students refer to the *Sixteenth Century* as the Renaissance.

Do not capitalize occupations unless used as a title before a proper name.

doctor
professor
nurse

Rod called the *doctor's* office and made an appointment with *Doctor* Hacker.

EXERCISE

Correct the use of capital or lower case letters in the following sentences.

1. I responded, "you will see me again."
2. Jerry took courses in history, spanish, chemistry, rhetoric, and biology I.
3. Last year the class read *One Flew Over The Cuckoo's Nest.*
4. His Mother gave him a Chevrolet station wagon.
5. My aunt Joan used to be a cartoonist.
6. Jason's sister played basketball with her Uncle at the High School.
7. I always went fishing in the Northern part of the state.
8. My son planned to go surfing in the Pacific ocean.
9. Amy took two courses in American literature.
10. The Stadium was located on Central street.

6
CLICHÉS `cl`

Clichés are stock phrases and figures of speech that have lost their suggestive value through overuse. In conversation we all use worn out expressions like *beat around the bush* without thinking about what they mean. Writers, however, have time to think, and they should use language meaningfully and imaginatively. The use of clichés in writing suggests that the author is too lazy or unimaginative to search for fresh and vigorous expressions. As you write, think about your word choice and choose exact and vivid words. Notice how clichés weaken the sentences in the following examples:

> The Hoyas *fought until the bitter end,* but finally they were defeated by the more experienced Tarheels. [weak]
>
> The Hoyas struggled until the final second, but finally they were defeated by the more experienced Tarheels. [stronger]
>
> The experienced Tarheels defeated the young Hoyas in the final seconds. [strongest]
>
> The entire team *worked like horses,* and now they *can stand tall,* even in defeat. [weak]
>
> The team played its best game of the season and all of the players are proud of their effort, even in defeat. [stronger]

Here is a brief list of clichés that have lost their value as fresh figures of speech:

> stitch in time
> no stone unturned
> a bull in a china shop
> apple of his eye
> sneaking suspicion
> ladder of success
> hit the nail on the head
> cool as a cucumber
> shot in the dark
> add insult to injury

ladder of success
straight as an arrow
blow off my last class

EXERCISE

Rewrite the sentences below to eliminate clichés.

1. His son, Harry, is a chip off the old block.
2. Part of the American dream is that the man in the street perceives his home is his castle.
3. Mary was as proud as a peacock that her son was hitting the books.
4. In this day and age people must get on the ball and learn a meaningful trade if they want to climb the ladder of success.
5. Last but not least, I found out that getting money from my uncle was like pulling teeth.

7
FAULTY COORDINATION coord

Coordination is the joining of two or more words, phrases, or clauses so that they have the same grammatical structure and importance. By coordinating the two grammatically equal elements, the writer is giving equal emphasis to each of them.

Generally, two or more simple sentences can also be advantageously combined by means of one of the *coordinating conjunctions: and, or, nor, for, but, yet,* and *so.* (See Part 2, p. 28.) Coordination can also be achieved through the use of conjunctive adverbs such as *however, nevertheless,* and *therefore.* (See also Part 2, pp. 28–29.) By joining (compounding) simple sentences, the writer shows a relationship that simple sentences alone cannot achieve.

The administration was sympathetic to the needs of the students. It did not recommend an increase in financial aid. [no relationship expressed]

The administration was sympathetic to the needs of the students, *yet* it did not recommend an increase in financial aid. [coordinating conjunction *yet* shows contrast]

The administration was sympathetic to the needs of the students; however, it did not recommend an increase in financial aid. [conjunctive adverb *however* shows contrast]

When you use a coordinating conjunction, be certain that it expresses the relationship that you intend to express. *And* would not express the intended relationship in the above example since it suggests addition rather than contrast. *For* would make a less meaningful relationship since it suggests cause.

Faulty coordination occurs most frequently in the situations described below.

Coordination of unrelated ideas

When two ideas do not seem to be related in fact, do not try to connect them.

FAULTY

My French class was at 8:00, and I failed the course. [no relationship]

REVISED

Since it is difficult for me to get up in the morning, I failed my 8:00 French class. [relationship expressed through subordination]

Excessive coordination

Avoid excessive coordination. Lengthy strings of compounded elements are monotonous to read.

FAULTY

My daughter spent last summer at the lake, and she worked as a waitress, and she saved enough to pay for her tuition.

REVISED

My daughter saved enough to pay for her tuition because she worked as a waitress at the lake last summer.

7 / Exercise   67 | coord

When you combine several sentences into one with coordinating conjunctions, you may find it helpful to change a sentence by omitting or adding words. The tendency merely to string thoughts together can be eliminated by a greater awareness of subordination, a technique used to indicate that one idea is not as important as the other.

Coordination is also discussed in Part 2, p. 28. You should study that section and Faulty Subordination, p. 153 in Part 3.

EXERCISE

Use the appropriate coordinating conjunctions to join the simple sentences below.

1. The chairman will send copies of the minutes to Frank. Sarah will distribute them.
2. The fabric may fade after several washings. It will not shrink.
3. The woman behind me wanted the bus window open. The man beside her wanted it closed.
4. The nursemaid was sleepy. She paid strict attention to the child.
5. Flying is a safe and fast means of transportation. I prefer travelling by automobile.

Use subordination to eliminate the problems with faulty coordination in the sentences below.

1. Jerry has been crippled since birth, and he has always wanted to be an athlete, so he entered a wheelchair marathon last year.
2. He picked up his pencil. He tried to jot down some ideas. His mind went blank.
3. The avalanche occurred last night, and none of the skiers were *was* → lost.
4. The campers could not find any dry kindling wood, and it rained yesterday.
5. We were walking home from school, and the storm kept getting worse, and a lady invited us to sit on her porch.

8
COMMA SPLICES [cs]

Independent clauses are simple sentences. When two or more of them are improperly joined with a comma, the result is a comma splice. When they are joined without a connector or appropriate punctuation, the result is a fused or run-on sentence. (See pp. 82–83 for a discussion of the fused sentence.)

Whenever a sentence contains two or more independent clauses, those clauses must be separated in one of these ways:

TWO SIMPLE SENTENCES
Mary went to the baseball game. Her husband went to the concert.

A SEMICOLON BETWEEN THE TWO CLAUSES
Mary went to the baseball game; her husband went to the concert.

A CONJUNCTIVE ADVERB BETWEEN THE CLAUSES
Mary went to the baseball game; however, her husband went to the concert.

NOTE: The conjunctive adverb should be preceded by a semicolon and followed by a comma.

A COMMA AND A COORDINATING CONJUNCTION
Mary went to the baseball game, and her husband went to the concert.

SUBORDINATION
Although her husband went to the concert, Mary went to the baseball game.

Note that all of the methods used above are grammatically correct. The one that you choose depends upon style and emphasis. Clearly the use of the period in the first example is the least desirable unless the ideas are only loosely related.

Remember, a comma alone is not sufficient punctuation for joining two independent clauses. If stronger punctuation is not used, the result is a comma splice.

Joe went to the hockey game, Cliff went to the tennis match. [incorrect]

Joe went to the hockey game; Cliff went to the tennis match. [correct]

For further discussion of the comma splice see the following sections:

Faulty Coordination (**coord**), p. 65
Fused or Run-on Sentences (**fs/RO**), p. 82
Uses of the Comma (**p/,**), p. 102
Uses of the Semicolon (**p/;**), p. 109
Faulty Subordination (**sub**), p. 153

EXERCISE

Revise the comma splices in each of the sentences below. Use each method of joining independent clauses at least twice (simple sentences, semicolon, conjunctive adverb, comma and coordinating conjunction, subordination).

1. The audience applauded, the critics did not.
2. I helped Joan, Norman drove to the office to get Barbara.
3. Amy made the motion, Rebecca seconded it.
4. Joel went water skiing in the morning, Matt went surfing in the afternoon.
5. Rod ate a pizza after he played his saxophone, Miki drank a beer after she played her flute.
6. Superman used to be a comic-strip character, now he is the star of two major movies.
7. We were very tired, we went to bed after midnight.
8. Joshua went to practice early, he came home late.
9. Wesley was married in 1975, his life has not been the same since.
10. Angela's favorite subject was accounting, David preferred art history.

9
DICTION d/dic

Correct diction or the appropriate use of language means the accurate choice of a word or words to express an idea. Writers have difficulty controlling their diction when they do not use care in choosing appropriate words. Diction should be correct, clear, and effective, but there are no absolute rules. There are some guidelines, however, that writers should learn to follow.

The audience is the most important factor in controlling diction. We may, for example, use slang in a letter to a close friend, but this would be inappropriate in a job application. Good writers must learn to adapt their language to a variety of audiences. In explaining to a child how an outboard motor operates, you do not use the language of a mechanical engineer. In most college courses, unless otherwise instructed, you can assume that your teacher and fellow students are your audience.

You should address your audience in a language that it is willing to understand and accept. Generally, your own judgment is your best guide as long as you have a distinct audience in mind. It is helpful to pretend that you are speaking directly to one member of that audience.

In addition, any good dictionary will tell you the level of usage of a particular word. The level of usage refers to the context in which a word is appropriate. If a word is not labeled in the dictionary, it is probably appropriate for standard written English. (This is not to say, however, that it is automatically the *most appropriate* word for your context.) If a word is labeled colloquial (colloq.), slang, or nonstandard (NS), it is inappropriate for standard written work unless you have made a stylistic choice to use it for special effect.

In selecting words writers should remember that

1. Words should be in current and general use.
2. Words should be in reputable use.
3. Words with appropriate denotations and connotations should be used to make diction precise.
4. Words should be concise.

Current and general use

Obsolete and archaic words and neologisms. Avoid obsolete and archaic words and some neologisms. *Obsolete* and *archaic* are both dictionary labels for words that have passed out of use. Neologisms, on the other hand, are words coined so recently that they have not yet come into established use.

> fain [archaic]
> signaturize [neologism — not acceptable]

It is interesting to note how rapidly language standards change:

> motor hotel [now archaic]
> motel [an acceptable neologism]

Regionalisms. Avoid regionalisms. Regionalisms are words or phrases that are used and understood primarily in a particular section of the country. Regionalisms are colorful, but they should be avoided in writing intended for general use. Here is an example of the confusion that may result:

> The mayor of Peabody ordered a cup of regular coffee. [In the Midwest regular coffee is black, but in New England it is served with cream.]

Technical words. Use technical words appropriately. Most frequently you are writing for a general audience, and your diction should convey that. In some special situations, however, technical language allows specialists to communicate efficiently. Without explanation, however, these technical words are meaningless to a general audience, and they should be avoided. If you must use technical terms, you should define them, as shown in the following examples.

> In warmer weather cross-country skiers will have to use klister (a soft wax) to prevent slipping.
> Eskimos wear mukluks (a high boot made of fur) in the cold season.

Pretentious writing. Avoid pretentious writing. Students have a tendency to try to write in a language that they think their instructor *wants* to hear. Instructors, however, want students to sound natural. They do not want students to use more or longer words than necessary. Here is an example of pretentious writing:

> Most institutions of higher education are eminently well-equipped for various recreational pursuits. [pretentious]
> Most colleges provide recreational facilities for their students. [standard]

Reputable use

Slang. Avoid slang. Most slang is narrow, flippant, and meaningful only to a special audience. It is usually too vague and imprecise for effective communication. Instructors object to slang because it has a limited audience and because it only approximates exact thought.

> Jason was *ripped* at his instructor when the grades were posted.
> In 1979 young people were really *getting into* disco.

NOTE: For additional information see Clichés, pp. 64–65.

Colloquial language. Be careful with colloquial language. Literally, colloquial English means conversational English. Colloquial expressions are a part of standard English, and they are acceptable in many writing situations; however, they may be glaringly out of place in formal and serious writing.

> The students and faculty council debated the issue of student representation for three hours. By the time the meeting adjourned, the *kids* felt that they had not been given a *good deal*.

Idioms. Be aware of problems with idioms. Idioms are expressions with arbitrary meanings different from the suggested meaning of the words themselves. Idiomatic English concerns words used in combination with others. Here are some examples:

ran across	plug away at	differ with
all thumbs	rub elbows with	differ from

Since people learn the idioms of their language naturally, idioms rarely pose a problem for native speakers. Most errors in English idioms occur in the use of prepositions after verbs. For example, *angry with a person,* is idiomatic and acceptable, whereas *angry at a person* is less acceptable. Most questions about idioms can be solved by consulting a good dictionary. The following are examples of common idioms used with prepositions that give writers problems:

CORRECT	LESS ACCEPTABLE
conform with a rule	conform to a rule
agree to a proposal	agree on a proposal
agree on a plan	agree to a plan
angry with	angry at
different from	different than
identical with	identical to
in accordance with	in accordance to
plan to	plan on

EXERCISE

Revise the problems with diction in the following sentences. Use C if you feel that a sentence is acceptable.

1. There is only one measly restaurant in the entire town.
2. Please signaturize this contract.
3. There are many viewers who consider the tube an insult to their intelligence.
4. Jack felt that his father was being too hard-nosed when he grounded him for a week.
5. Matt and Peter planned on going to the hot baths.
6. Arthur was really tuned into Medieval British History.
7. Bill argued that passivity is endemic in our student body.

8. Joanne could not study for the test because she was hung up on the first chapter.
9. Peggy ignored the hassle of class by not attending.
10. It's the same old story every time the Smiths come for a visit.

Denotation and connotation

Paying close attention to using words according to their denotations is the first rule of precise diction. When writers have selected a word that is acceptable in standard written English, they still have not solved the problem of word selection. They must now ask if the word they have chosen has the *denotative* and *connotative* values that they desire.

All words have denotation and most have connotation. To denote means "to point to" and to connote means "to imply." The denotation of a word is the thing or idea that it refers to — the meaning listed in the dictionary.

Looking for the precise word with the appropriate connotative value is the second rule of precise diction. Connotation includes all of the emotional overtones suggested by a word. Most writers select words with correct denotations, but they often have difficulty choosing the exact word they want by misjudging its connotation. Consider the following examples using the verb *walk*:

The student *walked* out of the room.
The student *ambled* out of the room.
The student *stormed* out of the room.
The student *sauntered* out of the room.

At the denotative level all four verbs are essentially the same in that they describe the act of leaving the room by means of one's feet and legs. At the connotative level, however, the four sentences suggest four quite different things. The first sentence is safe but less effective than the others because it is not very precise. The other three sentences are more precise and descriptive.

Finding the word with the appropriate connotative value is the writer's most challenging task. Although it often takes much time and effort, it can make the difference between flat and lively writing. Since by definition nouns and verbs dominate a sentence, it is often useful to go back over your writing and circle all of the verbs, for example. Ask yourself if each carries the weight that it should. Eliminate tired verbs like *walk*. Very often this process will make your writing more concise by substituting a simple verb, *stormed*, for a phrase, *walked angrily*.

Be concise

As you revise your writing, cross out all empty words and phrases and words that are repetitive. Many words and phrases in our language often serve little purpose other than filling space. Learn to recognize these fillers and eliminate them. Here are a few examples of filler phrases and their substitutes.

Filler phrase	Substitute
at that time	then
at this time	now
in the event that	if
the fact that	that
had come to a close	ended
in all cases	always
due to the fact that	because
it is often the case that	often
because of the fact	because

For a further discussion of concise and precise writing, see pp. 172–175.

EXERCISE

Make the diction more precise and concise in the following sentences. Use C if you feel that a sentence is acceptable.

1. Follow this advice in the event that the motor stops.
2. The children laughed as their father fell out of the canoe.
3. Due to the fact that many people don't care who wins the election, very few are expected to vote.
4. The smell of the city dump on a hot day is unbearable.
5. The angry student walked out of the room because of the fact that the teacher reprimanded him for laughing loudly.
6. The photography was lavish, but the movie itself was lousy.
7. Even senior citizens seem to be getting into board sailing.

8. Most small towns are not eminently well-equipped for the various recreational pursuits of senior citizens and teenagers.
9. In her job at the airport, Jessica got to rub elbows with some big wigs.
10. Rod was angry with his wife for burning the onion soup.

Explain the differences in connotation between the words in the groups below:

1. fanatical / enthusiastic
2. hoarded / saved
3. slim / skinny
4. crippled / handicapped
5. love / lust
6. stout / fat

10
DANGLING MODIFIERS   dm

An adjective or adverb phrase or clause that does not modify any word in a sentence is called a *dangling modifier*.

When the subject of the main clause is not modified by an introductory modifier, we say that the modifier dangles. Usually dangling modifiers are verbals placed at the beginning of the sentence. An introductory modifier (verbal or verbal phrase) must clearly modify the subject of the main clause that follows it.

FAULTY

Looking out the window, thoughts of his childhood came to him.

REVISED

Looking out the window, he thought of his childhood.

The problem to notice with the first example is that it says one thing but means something else. Clearly it is ridiculous to assume that thoughts of his childhood were looking out the window. To correct the dangling modifier we must do one of two things:

1. Make the subject of the main clause accept the modifier logically. In the revised example above the pronoun *he* serves this function and the modification is clear.
2. Change the introductory modifier into a complete clause.

    While he was looking out the window, thoughts of his childhood came to him.

Although there are no absolute rules for opening modifiers, writers should be particularly careful that all modifiers are clearly related to the rest of the sentence — probably the subject of the main clause.

For additional information see the discussion of verbal phrases in Part 2, p. 35.

EXERCISE

Revise the dangling modifiers in the following sentences. Try to use both methods of correction throughout the exercise by either modifying the subject of the main clause or changing the introductory modifier into a complete clause.

1. Having become a published author, Bob's life is unchanged.
2. Walking down the street, the driver of the red Corvette asked me directions.
3. Looking northward, the smoke from the paper mill blackened the horizon.
4. Reaching sixteen, Matt's interest changed from baseball to automobiles.
5. Running home from the theater, the taxi ran over the curb and nearly hit Lisa.
6. To become an effective writer, patience and precision are required.
7. Before going fishing, the boat was inspected.
8. Studying and worrying, my examination was a success.
9. To play basketball, coordination is essential.
10. By patching the cracked wall, our house was less drafty.

11
SENTENCE FRAGMENTS frag

A sentence fragment is a series of words that begins with a capital letter and ends with a period but does not contain an independent clause with a complete subject and predicate.

Every sentence must have at least one independent clause with a complete subject and predicate. Several sentence types consist of various combinations of phrases and dependent and independent clauses. A sentence fragment usually occurs when a dependent clause of a phrase is treated as a complete sentence. If you are having difficulty with sentence fragments, there are several things that you should do to stop alienating readers with this serious error. You should begin by studying the brief sentence grammar in Part 2, pp. 31–40 and then study the related sections in Part 3: Fused or Run-on Sentences, p. 82 and Comma Splices, p. 68. Also, you should practice reading your writing aloud because frequently writers can hear sentence fragments that they do not see.

Although the following list is by no means complete, most sentence fragments are from the types described below.

Appositive phrases

FAULTY

Bicycling strengthens the leg muscles, but also strengthens other parts of the body. For example, the lungs and the heart. [The nouns *lungs* and *heart* are in apposition with parts, and they cannot stand alone.]

REVISED

Bicycling strengthens the leg muscles, but it also strengthens other parts of the body — for example, the lungs and the heart.

Prepositional phrases

FAULTY

The long, winding road seemed treacherous. On stormy nights in particular. [The prepositional phrase beginning with *on* is an adverbial modifying *treacherous* and should be appropriately attached.]

11 / Sentence Fragments   79 | **frag**

REVISED
The long, winding road seemed treacherous, on stormy nights in particular.

Infinitive phrases

FAULTY
After much heated discussion with their parents, Kevin and Rachel finally received permission. To ride their motorcycles across the United States next summer. [The infinitive phrase beginning with *to ride* cannot stand alone and should not be separated from its main clause.

REVISED
After much heated discussion with their parents, Kevin and Rachel finally received permission to ride their motorcycles across the United States next summer.

Participial phrases

FAULTY
Jack spent all night looking for his pet raccoon. He finally found it as the sun was rising. Hiding behind the woodpile. [The participial phrase beginning with *hiding* modifies the word *it* and should be placed more closely to what it modifies. The phrase cannot stand alone as a sentence.]

REVISED
Jack spent all night looking for his pet raccoon. He finally found it hiding behind the woodpile as the sun was rising.

Dependent clauses

FAULTY
Indignant at the president, the treasurer stormed from the meeting. Although he never really gave the president a chance to explain himself. [The clause beginning with *although* does have a complete subject and predicate, but it cannot stand alone because the subordinating conjunction *although* forces it to be dependent upon the preceding independent clause.]

frag | 80 | An Alphabetical List of Frequent Writing Problems

REVISED

Indignant at the president, the treasurer stormed from the meeting, although he never really gave the president a chance to explain himself. [Note that without *although* this could be two simple sentences.]

Objective clauses

Objective (*who* or *which*) clauses often lead to problems with sentence fragments.

FAULTY

That is the person I was talking about. Who bumped into my car last night. [The pronoun *who* forces the second sentence to be dependent upon the first. It cannot stand alone.]

REVISED

That is the person I was talking about who bumped into my car last night.

NOTE: For further discussion of subordination see pp. 153–156.

Subject with no complete verb

FAULTY

My childhood home with its large kitchen, cozy dining area, and recreation room. [The subject *home* does not have a complete verb. Frequently modifiers interrupt the subject and verb position, and the writer forgets to include the verb.

REVISED

My childhood home with its large kitchen, cozy dining area, and recreation room is being converted into a duplex.

Permissible fragments

The use of sentence fragments is permissible in questions and answers in dialogue.

"How far is it to Flagstaff?"
"Fifty miles."

11 / Exercise   81 | frag

Sentence fragments can be used as exclamations and commands.

Ouch!

Go to your bedroom! [*You* is the understood subject.]

Sentence fragments can be used for stylistic emphasis. Experienced writers often use the sentence fragment to emphasize something. The first sentence in Charles Dickens' *Bleak House* is "London." The third sentence is "Implacable November weather."

Sentence fragments can also be used for transitions:

On to the next point.

EXERCISE

Revise each of the fragments below. Be prepared to explain why each is a fragment. Try listening for the fragments by reading the sentences aloud. Use C to designate a correct sentence.

1. The higher octane gasoline gives higher gas mileage, but so do other things. Like driving at a slower speed and inflating the tires with correct air pressure.
2. Sam wondered why his son became carsick so often. In the morning particularly.
3. The buffet featured many more entrees than roast beef and shrimp. For example, lobster Newburg, sweet and sour pork, and salmon.
4. We were an hour late for the baseball game; but when we finally arrived, we saw "Yaz." Getting his three-thousandth base hit.
5. Amy got a new blue blazer for her birthday. With corduroy knickers and a print blouse.
6. Jerry has always been afraid to walk past the cemetery near his house. On dark and windy nights in particular.
7. My favorite vacation spot, Cape Cod, with its sunny beaches, fine restaurants, and cool evenings.
8. Sharon spent the whole week arguing with her mother. On Friday her mother finally gave her permission. To go to the late movie after the game.

9. When David's car would not start, he was furious with his mechanic. Even though he ignored the warning about the worn battery cables.
10. Marie did not stay home much on weekends. Especially after she got a driver's license.

12
FUSED OR RUN-ON SENTENCES fs/RO

The fused or run-on sentence means that a writer has joined two independent clauses without punctuation or a coordinating conjunction. Fused sentences are not as common in writing as comma splices, but when they occur they are more of a problem for the reader. If writers were to proofread aloud, they might hear a natural pause between the two clauses and eliminate the problem.

> Larry Bird is a great basketball player he is also reserved and humble.

The natural pause is between *player* and *he*. If the writer places a comma after player, he will still have a problem because he has created a comma splice. Once the two independent clauses have been isolated, fused sentences can be joined in the same five ways that comma splices can:

TWO SIMPLE SENTENCES
Larry Bird is a great basketball player. He is reserved and humble.

SEMICOLON BETWEEN THE TWO CLAUSES
Larry Bird is a great basketball player; he is reserved and humble.

SEMICOLON AND CONJUNCTIVE ADVERB FOLLOWED BY A COMMA
Larry Bird is a great basketball player; nevertheless, he is reserved and humble.

COMMA AND COORDINATING CONJUNCTION
Larry Bird is a great basketball player, yet he is reserved and humble.

SUBORDINATION
Larry Bird is a great basketball player who is reserved and humble.

For further discussion of the fused or run-on sentence see the following sections:

Faulty Coordination (**coord**), p. 65
Comma Splices (**cs**), p. 68
Uses of the Comma (**p/,**), p. 102
Uses of the Semicolon (**p/;**), p. 109
Faulty Subordination (**sub**), p. 153

EXERCISE

Rewrite each of the fused sentences below. Use all five methods of correction for each sentence.

1. His girlfriend is a good cook she learned to cook as a child.
2. Guy's mother lives in Wisconsin she is eighty years old.
3. David and Peggy went on a bicycle trip they spent a night in a rustic inn.
4. The syllabus is not very clear it confuses many students.
5. The parking problem at the university is worse than last year students suggest a shuttle bus from the stadium.

13
USES OF THE HYPHEN hy

The hyphen is used as an aid in spelling; it is not a mark of punctuation, and it should not be confused with the dash. If you type your papers, the dash is made with two hyphens (--). (See Uses of the Dash, p. 113.) There are few absolute rules governing the use of the hyphen, so when in doubt, you should consult a good dictionary. As a general rule, the hyphen is used to divide words or to form compound words.

The most important functions of the hyphen are described below.

Compound expressions

Adjectives. Two or more words used as a single adjective before a noun are usually hyphenated.

> so-called police department
> fly-by-night business
> old-fashioned winter

Nouns. A compound noun is composed of two or more words that function as a single noun and should be hyphenated. (This rule also applies when a prefix retains its original strength in the compound.)

> anti-American
> pre-Christian
> X-ray
> shadow-boxing
> self-motivated
> merry-go-round

NOTE: Prefixes are usually hyphenated if they or the noun they precede are capitalized.

Fractions and compound numbers

Use a hyphen when writing numbers from twenty-one to ninety-nine. Fractions are also hyphenated.

> twenty-two
> one-half
> one-third

Word division

When dividing a word at the end of a line, use a hyphen. Hyphenate only between syllables and do not divide words of one syllable. Don't divide words before the adverb suffix *-ly* or the plural suffix *-es*. The hyphen only goes at the end of a line rather than at the beginning of the next line.

Preventing ambiguity

Make sure you hyphenate for correct meaning. Consider this phrase:

a package of five pound bags

It is not clear whether this refers to five bags weighing a pound each or bags weighing five pounds each.

five pound-bags
five-pound bags

EXERCISE

Hyphenate each of the following. Use C if the example is correct.

1. one fourth of the income
2. second-class citizen
3. one hundred-twenty-seven
4. small children's store
5. L-shaped room

Divide the following words:

1. rapid
2. grotesque
3. really
4. tenth
5. axes

14
ITALICS (UNDERLINING)   ital

In a typed or handwritten manuscript underline the word or phrase that would be italicized in print. Italics (underlining) are used in the situations discussed below.

Titles

Italicize (underline) the titles of books, magazines, newspapers, plays, long poems, movies, television programs, works of visual art and music.

ital | 86 An Alphabetical List of Frequent Writing Problems

The Bell Jar
Newsweek
Hill Street Blues
Beethoven's *Ninth Symphony*
the *Mona Lisa*

NOTE: Titles of brief works (short stories, songs, poems, book chapters, magazine and newspaper articles) are placed within quotation marks.

"A Rose for Emily"
"I Wandered Lonely as a Cloud"
"Lady"

NOTE: Copy the title of a newspaper as it appears on the masthead. Be careful with the article *the* — it may or may not be part of the title.

the *Los Angeles Times*
The New York Times

Names of vehicles

Italicize (underline) the names of ships, rockets, airplanes, and trains.

Spirit of St. Louis
Wabash Cannonball
Apollo XI

Foreign words and expressions

Italicize (underline) foreign words and expressions that have not become a part of English vocabulary.

déjà vu
fait accompli

Latin abbreviations are not italicized.

etc.   i.e.   et al.

Words, numbers, and figures

Italicize (underline) words, numbers, and figures that are referred to directly.

He had trouble pronouncing *unanimity*.
Change the *5's* to *6's*.
The word *Mississippi* has four *i's*.

Emphasis

You may italicize (underline) a word or phrase that you want to emphasize. Be sure to do this sparingly if you want it to be effective.

Use that telephone *only* in an emergency.

EXERCISE

In the following sentences underline all words that should be in italics in print and underlined when typed or handwritten. Use quotation marks where appropriate. Use C to designate a correct sentence.

1. The Orient Express may well be the most famous of all trains thanks to Agatha Christie's book Murder on The Orient Express.
2. Did you read Poe's The Fall of the House of Usher last year?
3. Do you remember the flight of Apollo I?
4. Open the door, s'il vous plait.
5. His grades were three A's and two B's.
6. The word relevant is difficult for me to spell.
7. Jeffery played in the orchestra for Mozart's The Magic Flute.
8. Last year the class read Frost's poem Stopping by Woods on a Snowy Evening.
9. The Boston Globe was the only newspaper Candice read. Newsweek was her favorite magazine.
10. Was your favorite record album Déjà Vu?

15
FAULTY LOGIC `log`

All expository writing involves reasoning because you are trying to convince your readers to accept what you have to say. To convince your readers that what you have to say is worth reading, make statements that are reasonable. Your writing must reflect clear, logical thinking. You are entitled to your own opinion, but be certain to present those opinions logically.

Writers often have trouble with logic in the situations discussed below.

Establishing a moderate tone

You will write more effectively if you are moderate in your judgment and diction. Dogmatism tends to alienate your readers. Avoid being overconfident and brash. Think carefully before you use such words as *appalling, atrocious, dreadful, fantastic, horrifying,* and *shocking.*

Supporting opinions with facts

When an opinion is stated without support, it is not convincing. Writers need to let their readers know what their evidence is and how it led to their opinion. An opinion must be verifiable. For example, if you know that thousands of people are murdered each year because handguns are too accessible, you may form the opinion that the sale of handguns should be controlled by the federal government. This is an opinion, and as such it is only your view on an issue. Other facts might lead people to other opinions. Let your readers know what evidence led you to your opinion.

Oversimplification

Most issues cannot be reduced to either/or solutions. Life just is not that simple. Try to offer a "middle ground" or compromise position. Avoid such reasoning as "Either we eliminate handguns in America through legislation or we acknowledge our indifference to the value of human life."

Hasty generalizations

Avoid jumping to a conclusion hastily after having observed only a few instances. A conclusion must be based on sufficient evidence. Consider the following statement:

15 / Faulty Logic

> Rock music is the cause of irresponsible behavior among teenagers.

The logic of the above statement is faulty because it does not account for other influences on the behavior of teenagers. This statement needs evidence, and obviously such proof would be impossible to find. It is reasonable, however, to say something like:

> The book *Parent Effectiveness Training* (*PET*) suggests that rock music may contribute to behavioral problems among teenagers. To support its position, *PET* says that . . .

Be certain to qualify your assertions by avoiding statements that involve *all, every, everything, none, always,* and *never* unless such words are accurate. It is better to use words like *some* or *many*.

All English teachers enjoy poetry. [no qualification]
Most English teachers enjoy poetry. [qualified]

Post hoc

Post hoc, ergo propter hoc is Latin for "after this, therefore because of this." This is a logical fallacy that assumes a cause and effect relationship between two facts simply because they follow one another.

John has the flu because he did not get a flu shot this year. [John's not getting a flu shot *may* be one of many reasons.]

The town should not have opened the youth center last month because three youths have been cited for possession of drugs since then. [It is incorrect to assume that the opening of the youth center contributed to the drug charges.]

Non sequitur

Non sequitur is Latin for "it does not follow." It is a common logical fallacy in which a conclusion does not follow from preceding statements.

Mike is the best runner I have seen this year. He will be selected to the All-State Team. [This assumes that the writer has seen all of the runners and that he is qualified to judge them.]

It is no wonder that today has been a bad day. I broke a mirror this morning.

False analogy

An analogy compares two things that are similar in one respect but dissimilar in others. False analogies obscure real issues. They should be used *only* to illustrate a point, never to prove it.

The possession of handguns was essential for our forefathers to protect themselves during the Westward expansion. If we are to remain true to the spirit of our ancestors, we must not allow ourselves to be deprived of our handguns. [This is not logical because it fails to consider the cultural and environmental differences between our society in two different phases of its historical development.]

Stereotypes

Stereotypes are rude and disrespectful caricatures of ethnic groups, social roles, and professions. A stereotype is not logical because it is a hasty and oversimplified characterization of a group of people.

A typical housewife, Sarah was interested only in her children and daytime television.

Ad hominem

Ad hominem means "to the man." When using this logical fallacy, the writer attacks the person rather than the issues.

That mechanic cannot fix my car — she's a woman!

Since the senator was treated for mental illness during the 1960s, we should not listen to his views on the next presidential candidate.

For further discussion of related topics see the following sections:

Diction (Denotation and Connotation) (**d/dic**), p. 74
Paragraph Unity (¶ **un**), p. 127
Paragraph Coherence (¶ **coh**), p. 131

EXERCISE

Identify the error in reasoning in each of the following and be prepared to discuss the reason for your choice.

1. The stocks were a deterrent to crime for our New England ancestors. Maybe a similar punishment should be employed today.
2. Joel's grades have dropped since he started dating Jennifer. He had better find a new girl friend.
3. It must be mentioned that this champion of highway safety has been convicted of driving while intoxicated.
4. College graduates have more social grace than people who have not graduated from college.
5. If we don't close the library before 11:00, the campus crime rate will continue to rise.
6. The university has a good faculty. All four of my teachers are excellent.
7. If we don't send military advisors into El Salvador, the Communists will take over the country.
8. He is a very wealthy man, so obviously he is against health insurance.
9. All guidance counselors are easy to talk with. I guess that's part of their job.
10. The crime rate rose during the mayor's administration. He was obviously not a "law and order" man.

16
MISPLACED MODIFIERS mm

Perhaps the most important quality of effective writing is clarity. Unclear writing often results when a writer does not place all adjective and adverb modifiers as close as possible to the words that they modify. Remember, an adjective or an adverb modifier can be a word, a phrase, or an entire clause. In each case it must be placed near the word it modifies. This discussion is closely related to the discussion of dangling modifiers in Part 3, pp. 76–77.

Writers who have problems with misplaced modifiers often reveal them in the situations discussed below.

Prepositional phrases and subordinate clauses

Prepositional phrases and subordinate clauses function as adjectives and adverbs. When they function as adjectives, they should be placed *directly* after the noun or pronoun that they modify. When they function as adverbs, they can be used in various places.

In each case make the modification clear. If you read your writing aloud, you can often hear misplaced modifiers.

FAULTY

Danny took his dog to the veterinarian that had a sprained ankle. [Obviously the dog and not the veterinarian has a sprained ankle.]

REVISED

Danny took his dog that had a sprained ankle to the veterinarian.

FAULTY

I spent last night talking about the stamps I had collected with my father. [A change in the position of the adjective prepositional phrase *with my father* will make the meaning clearer. As is, the sentence is ambiguous.]

REVISED

I spent last night talking with my father about the stamps I had collected.

Limiting adverbs

Place limiting adverbs like *only, just, almost,* and *simply* immediately before the word or word group they modify. Observe what happens with the position of the limiting adverb *only* in the following sentences:

I *only* spoke with the school nurse about my condition.

Only is misplaced because the above sentence has three possible interpretations:

1. *Only* I spoke with the school nurse about my condition.
2. I spoke *only* with the school nurse about my condition.
3. I spoke with the school nurse about my condition *only*.

The modifier is correctly placed in each of the three examples. Choose the position in the sentence that is consistent with your intended meaning.

Ambiguous (squinting) modifiers

Do not place a modifier so that it refers ambiguously to either the preceding or following word.

FAULTY

Anyone who watches television news *frequently* will notice that it is biased. [*Frequently* modifies either the verb *watches* or *will notice*. It must be moved.]

REVISED

Anyone who *frequently* watches television news will notice that it is biased.

REVISED

Anyone who watches television news will *frequently* notice that it is biased.

EXERCISE

Correct the misplaced modifiers in the sentences below. If a sentence has more than one interpretation, be prepared to discuss them all. Use C to designate a correct sentence.

1. My English instructor discussed why writers write sentence fragments on Tuesday.
2. Do you ever think that there will be peace in the Middle East?
3. Larry told the teacher with a straight face that he did his homework.
4. Jack bought some flowers in the store arranged in a basket.
5. Matthew promised when he came home that he would shovel the snow.
6. Wendy went to see the doctor who had a broken finger.
7. We planned to live in Scotland for six months.

8. Ruby just read one chapter for her chemistry class.
9. John entered his father in the race who can run a four hour marathon.
10. The mayor implied that he would present his new plan on television last night.

17
MANUSCRIPT FORM   ms

Your writing begins to make an impression upon your readers the moment that they look at the manuscript. A sloppy or unprofessional appearance will make your readers less receptive to what you have to say. Indeed, in the case of manuscripts, first impressions are lasting. Crossed out words and pages ripped from a spiral notebook suggest that you really don't care very much about your writing.

In general, you should follow the directions that your instructor gives for manuscript form. If you do not receive such directions, use the suggestions that follow as a guide for your final draft.

Typed papers

If you have a typewriter and can type, it is good practice to type all papers that you write out of class. No matter how legible your handwriting, typed manuscript is easier to read. Follow the suggestions below when typing.

1. Use unlined 8½- by 11-inch paper. Do not use onionskin paper.
2. Double-space throughout your paper. Quotations longer than four lines should be indented five spaces from the left margin and double-spaced. Triple-space before and after the quotation.
3. Center your title about two inches from the top of the page. Do not underline your title or close it in quotation marks unless it is itself a quotation. Leave one space between the title and the first line of your text.
4. Leave a one-inch margin on the left and right side of your page. The margin on the bottom should also be one inch.

5. Indent each paragraph five spaces from the left-hand margin.
6. Use two hyphens to make a dash with no spaces preceding or following. Leave two spaces after the colon and all end punctuation (period, question mark, and exclamation point). Leave one space after internal punctuation (comma, semicolon, and period after abbreviation).
7. Sign your papers as instructed. Include all of the information that is asked for, and put it in the upper right-hand corner of the first page unless otherwise instructed.
8. Number all pages except the first with an arabic numeral in the upper right-hand corner.

Handwritten papers

If you are writing your paper in longhand, follow these suggestions:

1. Use wide-lined 8½- by 11-inch white composition paper. Do not hand in pages that have been torn from a spiral-bound notebook because their edges stick together. Use black or blue ink.
2. Do not use narrow-ruled paper. Try to use the wide-ruled composition paper and write on every line. Do not write on the back of the pages.
3. Center your title on the top line and leave an extra space between the title and the first line of your text. Do not underline your title or close it in quotation marks.
4. Leave a one-inch margin on the left and right sides of the page. The margin on the bottom should also be one inch.
5. Indent each paragraph one inch from the left-hand margin.
6. Number all pages except the first with an arabic numeral in the upper right-hand corner.

Proofreading and corrections

Try to put your draft aside for awhile before you proofread it. This will make you a more objective critic of your own work. Changes and corrections should be kept to an absolute minimum to assure a neat final copy. If you find many mistakes, prepare another draft. For minor changes, make the corrections neatly. Here are some suggestions for correcting your final draft.

1. To add a word, use a caret (∧). Write the omitted word directly above it.

   Type your manuscript if ∧can. *(you inserted)*

2. To cancel a word, draw a single line through it. If it is a spelling error, write the correction above.

   Type your manuscript if ~~you~~ you can.

   Leave a one-inch left ~~margen~~. *(margin)*

3. To indicate the beginning of a new paragraph use the paragraph symbol (¶) before the first word of the new paragraph.

4. Use a curved line to show that two letters should be reversed.

   C*o*(mp)*o*se a title. Don't just state a topic.

18
ERRORS IN THE USE OF NUMBERS `num`

There are no absolute conventions for writing out numbers and using figures. The most important guideline in handling numerals is to be consistent. In most general writing numbers are usually written. Although usage varies, the following rules will serve as a guide for general writing:

Use figures for numbers that require more than two words to write out. Generally write out all numbers between one and one hundred. Remember, a hyphenated number is treated as one word.

The municipal debt was twenty-two million dollars.
There are 366 days in a leap year.

Do not begin a sentence with a number that is not spelled out.

Two hundred and eighty-nine people attended the school meeting.

If you are using a series of figures in a sentence, use numerals for them all.

The number of building permits issued during the past five years was 49, 36, 119, 99, and 122.

19 / Faulty Parallelism   para//

Use numbers for dates, addresses, page numbers, volume numbers, decimals, fractions, percentages, and time of day.

January 24, 1967
197 B.C.
385 Chapman Road
Volume 22
99.5%
$14\frac{1}{4}$
2:45 A.M.

EXERCISE

Correct the use of numbers in each of the following sentences. Use C to designate a correct sentence.

1. $3.50 was the admission fee.
2. On their vacation last summer, David and Peggy spent $890.
3. The show begins at 9:00 P.M.
4. He ran 14½ miles.
5. Peggy saved 145 dollars.
6. Look it up in Volume Twenty-one of the *World Book*.
7. The Newkirks moved to RFD 3, Mason City, Iowa.
8. A yard is thirty-six inches.
9. Christmas shopping cost us five hundred dollars.
10. I read it in Matthew, Chapter Two, Verse Three.

19
FAULTY PARALLELISM   para//

The principle that controls parallel structure is that when two or more items are equal in emphasis, they should be similar in grammatical structure. You should, for example, use nouns with nouns, infinitives with infinitives, and prepositional phrases with prepositional phrases. Parallel structure is desirable because it makes your writing consistent, balanced, and neat. It also signals your reader, thus making your writing easier to follow. In the sentence below the three parts of the compound predicate are balanced, coordinated, and parallel.

Students in college composition classes are taught to organize their thoughts, to supply specific information, and to write in complete sentences.

Notice the balance created by joining the three infinitive phrases. The use of the infinitive marker *to* assists the reader. Now observe what happens when there is a violation in parallel structure.

Students in college composition classes are taught to organize their thoughts, to supply specific information, and that they should write in complete sentences.

The series of two infinitive phrases is disrupted with the subordinate clause. The above sentence is not parallel because the coordinating conjunction *and* joins an infinitive phrase with a clause beginning with *that*.

Coordinating conjunctions *and, but, or, nor, for, so,* and *yet* are signals that parallel structure should be used.

The representatives often promise improved highways but rarely support legislation for highway maintenance.

The conjunction *but* joins the parallel predicates. In the sentence below the conjunction *and* coordinates the three prepositional phrases.

Maurice likes to read at home, at school, and at the office.

Writers should be especially conscious of parallelism when using the four pairs of correlative conjunctions:

both . . . and
either . . . or
neither . . . nor
not only . . . but also

I have *neither* the inclination *nor* the time to go jogging.
You can study for the midterm *either* at the library *or* at the student union.

For further discussion of parallel structure see the following section:

Faulty Coordination (**coord**), p. 65

20 / Uses of the Period

EXERCISE

Correct the errors in faulty parallelism in the following sentences. Use C to designate a correct sentence.

1. She was a collector, a spinster, and egotistical.
2. The teacher in the one-room school was required to teach subjects, to supervise play, and acting as an administrator as well.
3. Vickie could not decide whether to jog in the park or to bicycle to the next town.
4. Carol has become proficient at cross-country skiing and learning how to ride a motorcycle.
5. This semester Bob is studying French, biology, calculus, and how to deliver a speech.

Sections 20–30 deal with the various kinds of punctuation. They are not listed alphabetically because of the relationship of all types of punctuation, but are discussed here as a unit.

20
USES OF THE PERIOD p/.

Ends of sentences

Use the period at the end of a declarative or imperative sentence.

Writers should end a sentence with a period like this. [declarative sentence]

Mild commands and indirect questions

Use a period after mild commands and indirect questions.

Place a period after a mild command. [mild command]
The teacher asked why I couldn't define an indirect question. [indirect question]

Abbreviations

Use a period after most abbreviations.

Mr.   M.D.
Ms.   Ph.D.

p/? An Alphabetical List of Frequent Writing Problems

    A.M.   etc.
    P.M.   A.D.

(For a detailed discussion of the proper use of abbreviations, see p. 62.)

Acronyms. Periods are not used for abbreviations that are acronyms. (An acronym is a word that is formed by combining the initial letter or letters in each word of an organization's title or a process.)

    NATO
    GOP
    UNICEF

Popular abbreviations. Periods are usually not used with popular abbreviations for organizations and agencies.

    PTA
    IBM
    SALT (talks)

Quotation marks

Periods are always placed inside quotation marks.

    Sam said, "The car keys are on the table."

21
USES OF THE QUESTION MARK   p/?

Direct questions

Use a question mark after a direct question.

    Who will leave early?
    Where is the city park?

Use a period for indirect questions.

    The officer asked who had been creating the disturbance.

(See also p. 99 of this Part.)

Quotation marks

When a question ends the quoted part of a sentence, the question mark goes inside the quotation mark. If the entire sentence is a question, place the question mark after the quotation mark.

"Who has been creating this disturbance?" the officer asked.
The officer asked, "Who has been creating this disturbance?"
Did you say, "Who has been creating this disturbance"?

Parentheses

A question mark may be used in parentheses (?) to indicate doubt or uncertain information. Use this device sparingly.

Becky's grandfather was born in 1914 (?).

For further discussion of the question mark see the following section:

Uses of Quotation Marks (p/" "), p. 117

22
USES OF THE EXCLAMATION POINT p/!

Most typewriters do not have a separate key for the exclamation point. If you need to make one, type an apostrophe above a period (!).

Exclamation points are appropriate only after statements that would be given heavy stress when spoken.

Leave this office at once!

When Amy discovered that she had done the wrong assignment, she shouted, "Oh, no!"

NOTE: The exclamation point is a mark of end punctuation, and it does not need to be followed by a period.

Use the exclamation point sparingly. The exclamation point is usually not used in expository writing. Do not use it to accentuate a flat statement or to show sarcasm.

The judge told the convicted arsonist that he was going to give him a little (!) punishment. [incorrect]

If the exclamation is part of quoted material, place it inside quotation marks. Otherwise, place it outside.

> The pilot shouted, "Prepare for an emergency landing!"
> Don't say "ain't"!

EXERCISE

The following exercise is for all end punctuation. Correct the sentences for the appropriate use of periods, question marks, and exclamation points. Use C to designate a correct sentence.

1. The professor asked the student in the front row where the papers were?
2. His flight left promptly at 2:15 AM.
3. Please move the car that is blocking the entrance!
4. We will never yield to the demands of the union!
5. Larry used to wish that he were a salesman for IBM.

23 USES OF THE COMMA

The comma is the most widely used mark of punctuation. Accordingly, it is also the most widely misused. As a general rule, the comma is used to join elements within a sentence or to signal an interruption in the flow of the main clause. A pause often signals when a comma should be used in written work. Since we may "hear" when a comma should be used, proofreading aloud may be helpful. It is important to know the conventions governing the use of the comma. Remember that the primary function of the comma is to make a sentence clear.

The most frequent uses of the comma are discussed below.

Independent clauses

Use a comma to separate independent clauses. When two independent clauses are joined by a coordinating conjunction (*and, but, or, for, nor, so, yet*) a comma should be placed *before* the conjunction.

> Seattle is the largest city in Washington, and it is the gateway to Alaska and the Far East.

Sculptors use many elements found in painting, but a painter can give only an illusion of depth.

If the independent clauses are very short, you may omit the comma.

The organ sounded and the congregation rose.

Elements in a series

Use a comma to separate words, phrases, or clauses in a series. A comma should be used to separate three or more elements in a series.

The physical fitness instructor emphasized dancing, running, and bicycling.

The successful tennis player is one who practices all year, concentrates on each match, and challenges players better than himself.

NOTE: When the last element is joined to the series by a conjunction, place a comma before the conjunction. This helps the reader see that the two items are separate.

EXCEPTION: When the items in the series or clauses that are being joined are lengthy and complicated, containing commas themselves, they are usually separated by semicolons. (See Uses of the Semicolon, p. 109.)

The wood from the redwood tree is soft, red, and weak; but it is able to resist decay, insect damage, and weather.

Coordinate adjectives

Use a comma to separate coordinate adjectives. Adjectives that modify the same noun and can be joined by *and* or that can be reversed without changing the meaning are coordinate adjectives.

Bicycles provide inexpensive, efficient transportation. [Each adjective modifies transportation: *inexpensive, efficient* transportation.]

In the example above, one could just as easily say

efficient, inexpensive transportation

If an adjective is closely linked with a noun, the adjective is probably not coordinate with the adjective that precedes it.

a lengthy summer vacation [*Summer* and *vacation* are closely linked. *Summer* and *lengthy* are not coordinate with each other. *Lengthy* modifies summer vacation.]

A comma is not used between the final coordinate adjective and the noun.

inexpensive, efficient, transportation [incorrect]
inexpensive, efficient transportation [correct]

Numbers are not coordinate with other adjectives, and they are not separated by commas.

The audience listened to two long, boring speeches.

Introductory elements

Use a comma to set off introductory words, phrases, and clauses. This rule prevents misreading. The introductory elements modify a word or words in the independent clauses that follow:

Underneath, the desk was rotten.
Upstairs, the house was not finished.
Because he was perhaps America's greatest president, Franklin D. Roosevelt's one-hundredth birthday was remembered with a three-hour television special.
After becoming independent of architecture, sculpture became a unique art unto itself.
In other words, you did not pay the rent.

It is acceptable to omit the comma with short introductory elements.

By 1987 he will have left the country.
In Boston the seafood is always fresh.

Be careful not to confuse the reader. Use a comma when in doubt. Notice the confusion that results in the following examples:

When it was his turn to hit the pitcher took off his jacket.
After eating the workers returned to the assembly line.

Nonrestrictive modifiers and appositives

Use a comma to set off nonrestrictive modifiers and appositives. A dependent clause, participial phrase, or appositive that can be omitted without changing the main idea of the sentence is nonrestrictive. Nonrestrictive elements add additional — but not essential — information about the nouns that they modify. Restrictive elements are essential to the meaning of the sentence and essential to the identification of the noun that they follow. Frequently, writers must use their judgment as to whether an element is essential to the meaning or not. A good test is to read the sentence without the element in question. If the sentence makes essentially the same point, the element is probably nonrestrictive and should be set off by commas.

The following modifier is nonrestrictive because the essential meaning is still the same without the clause *which is the oldest home in town*. The *which* clause adds information, but it does not restrict the subject.

The Wheeler House, which is the oldest house in town, is open for visitors on Saturdays.

The following *which* clause restricts the subject houses to a specific type of house — old.

Several other houses which are also old are not open for visitation.

The italicized clauses in the following sentences are restrictive. Without them, the meanings of the sentences are substantially changed. Do not set off restrictive elements with commas.

The contestant *from the Soviet Union* broke the high jump record. [The phrase *from the Soviet Union* limits the noun *contestant* and is restrictive.]

Rod *often* thought of moving to another house. [*Often* limits the verb *thought* and is restrictive.]

The umpire read *from the rulebook* that leaving the base before the ball is pitched is not allowed in Little League baseball. [*From the rulebook* limits the verb read and is restrictive.]

An *appositive* is a noun or noun substitute that further describes a noun immediately preceding it. An appositive is usually nonrestrictive.

> Frank, my neighbor, plays golf every Wednesday.

NOTE: An abbreviated title or degree is treated as an appositive when it follows a proper name.

> Robert O'Connor, Ph.D., spoke in honor of James Joyce's birthday.
> David Gilmour, M.D., opened a new office in February.

Parenthetic elements and transitional words

Use a comma to set off interruptions — parenthetic elements and transitional words. Parenthetic words or phrases are intrusive and subordinate in a sentence. They interrupt the normal sentence pattern to supply supplementary information. They should be set off by commas.

> The book, as you can see, is in the stacks.
> To be sure, the student should be given a voice in the matter.

Adjectives that are inserted in other than their regular position before a noun are parenthetic.

> The old lady, tired and cross, chased the children from her property.

Transitional expressions like *indeed, however, consequently, accordingly, as a result of, in fact* are set off by commas unless they join two independent clauses. (See Uses of the Semicolon, p. 109.)

> The behavior of the mayor, for example, did not help the reputation of local politicians.
> In fact, the behavior may have destroyed it.

Mild interjections and direct address

Use a comma to set off *yes* and *no*, mild interjections, and words of direct address.

> No, my daughter cannot babysit next weekend.
> Jimmy, please pass the pepper.

Absolute phrases

Use a comma to set off absolute phrases. An absolute phrase is an introductory phrase consisting of a participle with a subject. It should be set off by commas. (See Part 2, p. 36.)

The storm having stopped, the bathers went back in the pool.

Dates, addresses, letter forms, and long numbers

Use commas correctly with dates, addresses, letter forms, place names, and numbers. In dates, separate the day of the month from the year and separate the date from the rest of the sentence.

July 6, 1940

On December 31, 1982, Amy and Lori had too much to drink.

The comma is optional when only the month and year are given.

January, 1967

January 1967

Separate numbers into thousands and millions.

1,000

25,000

1,650,000

In place names and addresses, separate items in addresses with commas and the final element from the rest of the sentence.

255 West Fountain Avenue, Delaware, Ohio 43015

Bill moved to Delaware, Ohio, having been born in Cleveland.

NOTE: There is no comma between the state name and the zip code.

In friendly letters a comma should follow the salutation and in all letters a comma should follow the complimentary close.

Dear Tracy,

Sincerely,

p/, | 108 An Alphabetical List of Frequent Writing Problems

Quotations

Use a comma to introduce a direct quotation and around quotation expressions such as *he said.*

Roosevelt said, "The only thing we have to fear is fear itself."
"When I was a student," he said, "I had to walk to school every day."

(See Uses of Quotation Marks, p. 117, for more information about quotation marks.)

For further discussion of the comma see the following sections:

Part 2, Sentences, pp. 31–40
Comma Splices (**cs**), p. 68
Fused or Run-on Sentences (**fs/RO**), p. 82
Uses of the Semicolon (**p/;**), p. 109

EXERCISE

Insert commas where they are required in the following sentences. Be prepared to give a reason for your choice.

1. Before the Renaissance most sculpture was planned and created in association with architecture.
2. When Michelangelo carved his statue of David he had no site in mind for the work.
3. The art of painting is associated with visual perception and the art of sculpture is associated with tactile sensation.
4. Great modern sculptors including Rodin and Moore emphasize feelings of thrust and pressure.
5. Today sculptors construct objects of steel iron concrete and plastic.
6. Relief sculpture gives an impression of objects occupying space but most sculpture is three-dimensional.
7. Modern sculptures like architecture define space rather than occupy it.
8. In classical sculpture drapery hung straight and stiffly.

24 / Uses of the Semicolon 109 p/;

9. Early Chinese sculptures were small stone figures placed in tombs
10. Primitive man recognized forms of living things in bones animal horns and rocks.
11. Eventually the Greeks who thought of their gods as being like men began to make sculpture of real people.
12. Michelangelo the best known sculptor of the Italian Renaissance is known for the deep feeling and emotion of his figures.
13. Today some sculptors follow the classic tradition some distort and exaggerate the human figure and some are more interested in problems of pure form.
14. As a result the human figure which has been an inspiration to sculptors for centuries has become less important.
15. The machine with its wheels chains and bolts has influenced artistic development.

Insert commas where they are required in the following items:

1. 34 Beacon Street Boston Massachusetts 02106
2. 1572686
3. James Squires M.D.
4. Dear Peggy
5. February 1982

24
USES OF THE SEMICOLON p/;

The semicolon is a stronger mark of internal punctuation than the comma. Like the period, it signals a complete pause, but it is used within a sentence to join coordinate elements. The semicolon is used in the situations described below.

Independent clauses

Use a semicolon to join independent clauses that are not connected with a comma and a coordinating conjunction. The coordinating conjunctions in English are *and, but, or, for, nor, so,* and *yet.*

p/;   110   An Alphabetical List of Frequent Writing Problems

The redwood tree thrives in the damp climate near the Pacific Ocean, and it rarely grows farther than fifty miles inland. [comma and coordinating conjunction]

The redwood tree thrives in the damp climate near the Pacific Ocean; it rarely grows farther than fifty miles inland. [no coordinating conjunction]

NOTE: If you use only a comma without a coordinating conjunction, you have produced a comma splice. (See Comma Splices, p. 68.)

Conjunctive adverbs

Conjunctive adverbs should be preceded by a semicolon and followed by a comma. Words like *however, moreover, nevertheless, consequently, therefore, indeed,* and *in fact* are conjunctive adverbs (transitional words). These words show transitions in thought between two related main clauses.

You must use your passbook each time you make a deposit; otherwise, you will never know how much money is in your account.

Rock music is played all over the world; however, Americans still play more rock than anyone else.

Often the conjunctive adverb can be moved to other positions in the sentence. When it is moved, put commas before and after the adverb.

Rock music is played all over the world; Americans, however, still play more rock than anyone else.

Long and complex clauses

Use a semicolon before a coordinating conjunction when the two main clauses are long and contain commas within.

The wood from a redwood tree is soft, red, and weak; but it is able to resist decay, insect damage, and weather.

Items in a series

Use a semicolon when some or all of the items in a series contain commas. This will enable your reader to easily determine

24 / Exercise   111 p/;

which are the major stopping points and which are less important.

The winning essays were written by students from Cleveland, Ohio; Springfield, Massachusetts; and Seattle, Washington.

For further discussion of the semicolon see the following sections:

Part 2, Sentences, pp. 31–40
Comma Splices, (cs), p. 68
Fused or Run-on Sentences, (fs/RO), p. 82
Uses of the Comma, (p/,), p. 102

EXERCISE

Review the comma rules in Uses of the Comma, p. 102, before you attempt this exercise. Use the comma and semicolon to punctuate the following sentences. Use C to designate a correct sentence.

1. An hour later the deck collapsed our digging had weakened the supports.
2. The Jacksons arrived at the motel with John, their six-year-old son, Debbie, their three-year-old daughter, and Casey, their six-month-old Irish Setter.
3. The lowest branches of a redwood tree may be eighty feet above the ground; but those of young trees grow all the way to ground level.
4. For thousands of years man has used refrigeration to preserve food but it has been widely used only since the mid-1800's.
5. Refrigeration removes heat from solids, liquids, and gases, and it is based on a law that states that heat flows from warmer to colder bodies.
6. The chairman's explanation seemed quite reasonable to me, however, the treasurer was still leery.
7. The Bactrian camel has two humps, the dromedary has one.
8. When people lack power to produce other methods of refrigeration; they cool with ice.
9. The Mainella's new house has a game room with a fireplace, a pool table, and a dart board, a living room with a picture

window, built-in bookcases, and a stereo cabinet, and a kitchen with a counter island, a food processor, and a microwave oven.
10. Jake was sick on Christmas Eve, however he still went to church at midnight.

25
USES OF THE COLON p/:

The colon is a formal mark of punctuation used primarily to introduce a list, a formal quotation, or an explanatory statement. (In typed papers, skip two spaces after the colon.)

Lists of appositives

Use a colon to introduce a list of appositives that ends an otherwise grammatically complete sentence. (Often such lists are introduced by *the following* or *a number*.)

The instructor found three major weaknesses in Judy's paper: sentence structure, spelling, and diction.

The sentence preceding the colon must be grammatically complete. (Do not separate the verb from its complements.)

My three favorite courses are: math, English, and German. [Incorrect use of colon to separate verb from complements.]

Formal quotations

A colon should be used to announce a formal quotation.

The Red Cross officially issued an urgent appeal: "Cots, canned food, and warm clothing are desperately needed in the stricken area."

Explanations

Use a colon to introduce an explanatory statement.

According to the swimming coach, there was only one thing we could do to win the meet: place in three of the last four events.

Business letters
Use a colon after a formal salutation in business letters.

Gentlemen:
Dear Mrs. Robinson:

Titles and subtitles
Use a colon between titles and subtitles.

Long Memory: *The Black Experience in America*

Other uses
Use a colon in the separation of hours and minutes in time and of chapter and verse in biblical citations.

9:45
Matthew 2:1–5

EXERCISE

Use the colon correctly in the following sentences. If the sentence is correct, mark it with C and be prepared to explain why it is correct.

1. There were many activities planned for the reunion: softball, windsurfing, swimming, and eating.
2. When the senator was recognized, he made his position clear, "Under no circumstances will I support the reelection of the president."
3. The teacher wore the same clothes everyday: a drab corduroy sportcoat and blue denim pants.
4. The three most important functions of the Red Cross are: health service, aid to veterans, and relief work.

26
USES OF THE DASH   p/ —

The dash is a dramatic mark of punctuation. It is used much like the comma and parentheses to separate an element from the rest of the sentence. The difference lies in the fact that the dash emphasizes that which is separated from the main clause. On a typewriter a dash is made with two hyphens with no spaces between (--). The dash is most commonly used in the following situations.

Interruptions and parenthetic elements

Use a dash to emphasize and set off abrupt interruptions and parenthetic elements.

Cardiologists recommend that young people — and middle-aged people for that matter — do aerobic exercises.

Use a dash to emphasize and set off parenthetic and other nonrestrictive elements.

The Reformation was a religious movement — social and political as well — that gave birth to Protestantism.

Winter in New England — with its cold, clear days and deep snow — is my favorite season.

In the 1500s many Protestant religious groups competed with the Catholic Church — and with each other — for the allegiance of Europeans.

Summary statements

Use a dash to set off an expression that summarizes a preceding statement.

Martin Luther criticized what he considered to be abuses of the Catholic Church — the sale of indulgences, and the intervention of a mortal between man and his God.

Introductory substantives

Use a dash to set off a series of introductory substantives (pre-subject appositives).

Anabaptists, Anglicans, Huguenots, and Presbyterians — these were among the many reform groups of the Reformation.

NOTE: The dash is an emphatic mark of punctuation, and it should be used with discretion. The dash should not be used in the

27 / Uses of Parentheses and Brackets   115   p/( )   [ ]

place of parentheses or commas. Parentheses deemphasize what they set off; commas set off neutrally.

NOTE: Dashes must always appear outside of quotation marks.

Poe's "The Fall of the House of Usher" — the instructor's favorite short story — uses a first-person narrator who is driven to madness.

For further discussion of related topics see the following sections:

Uses of the Comma, (p/,), p. 102
Uses of the Colon, (p/:), p. 112
Uses of Parentheses and Brackets, (p/( )   [ ]), p. 115

EXERCISE

Explain the use of the dash in the following sentences by citing the reason(s) for the use of the dash in each one.

1. The high cost of living — inflation had risen to fifteen percent — became the nation's most serious domestic problem.
2. Two players — Frank Robinson and Henry Aaron — were elected to the Baseball Hall of Fame.
3. Milk, eggs, bacon, and muffins — these are John's favorite breakfast foods.
4. Nancy Jenson — a girl who used to be very shy — is the public relations director for the new radio station.
5. There is only one kind of food that Matthew refused to eat — anchovies.

27
USES OF PARENTHESES AND BRACKETS   p/( )   [ ]

Parentheses

Like the dash and the comma, parentheses are used to separate or set off one element from the rest of the sentence. The three marks of punctuation, however, are quite different. The dash emphasizes the nonrestrictive element, the comma sets it off in a conventional manner, and parentheses deemphasize it. Parentheses should be used sparingly. They are most frequently used in the following situations.

Nonessential material. Use parentheses to enclose nonessential explanations and examples.

> Rembrandt (unlike many other artists) wrote almost nothing about his art.

Details and examples. Use parentheses to enclose details and examples.

> Rembrandt (1606–1669) was the greatest artist from the Netherlands.
>
> The profit margin in 1981 exceeded that of 1979 (see Table 1).

Figures in a series. Use parentheses to enclose figures used to list points.

> Rembrandt's reputation rests upon (1) his ability to show the feelings of people, (2) his use of light and shadow, and (3) his sensitivity to nature.

Brackets

Brackets are most frequently used in the situations described below.

Direct quotes. Use brackets to set off any information added to directly quoted material.

> The sportscaster said, "The NBA franchise in Boston [with its old arena] is the most successful in the nation." [*With its old arena* is an editorial comment that has been added to the direct quotation.]

Sic. Use brackets to set off [sic]. [Sic] is Latin for "in this manner." In brackets it indicates that an error existed in the original quotation.

The senator said, "The disposal of nuclear waste is not a relavant [sic] issue." [*Relevant* is spelled incorrectly.]

For further discussion of related topics see the following:

Uses of the Comma, (p/,), p. 102
Uses of the Dash, (p/ —), p. 113

EXERCISE

Explain the use of parentheses and brackets in the following sentences by citing one of the reasons given in the discussion above.

1. Only two of the teachers (both from the foreign language department) went to the documentary on travel.
2. Joel tipped over in a kayak (Eskimo canoe) on his vacation.
3. The missionary said, "Christianity (with over a billion [sic] followers) is the most widespread religion in the world."
4. Fish and chips are only one pound (about two dollars) in Edinburgh.
5. My history teacher said, "Judaism was one of the first religions in the world [Western world] to emphasize the belief in one God (monotheism)."
6. After graduation, the senior class planned (1) to charter an excursion boat, (2) to attend a play, and (3) to sponsor a party.

28
USES OF QUOTATION MARKS p/" "

Quotation marks are used primarily to enclose material that is directly quoted from printed sources or from dialogue. They are also used around titles of shorter works and to enclose words used in special, ironical senses. Quotation marks are used most frequently in the situations described below.

Direct quotations

Use quotation marks to enclose a direct quotation. Do not use quotation marks to enclose an indirect quotation — a paraphrase or report of what someone said.

The lifeguard said, "Stay out of the pool for an hour." [direct quotation]

"It's important," the lifeguard said, "for you to stay out of the pool for an hour." [direct quotation]

The lifeguard said that we should stay out of the pool for an hour. [indirect quotation]

Long quotations

When writing a long paper, you may use a direct quotation of several sentences or even several paragraphs. If the quotation is not interrupted by expressions like *he said,* use one set of quotation marks. (Do not put quotation marks around each sentence.) If the quotation is several paragraphs long, put quotation marks at the beginning of each paragraph. However, quotations of more than four lines are usually set off in most expository writing (see the sections below).

Dialogue, poetry, and lengthy prose passages

When quoting dialogue, begin a new paragraph with each new speaker.

"What did you expect to happen?"
"Nothing, I didn't think it would be so horrendous."
— Philip Roth

More than two lines of quoted poetry should be set off.

To set off, indent the verse five spaces from the left margin and double space. You do not need quotation marks when you set off the material.

The last stanza of Robert Frost's "Stopping by Woods on a Snowy Evening" has received much critical attention:

The woods are lovely, dark and deep.
But I have promises to keep,
And miles to go before I sleep,
And miles to go before I sleep.

Quoted verse of one or two lines may be run into the text of your paper. If you are quoting two lines, use a slash to separate the lines.

"The woods are lovely, dark and deep./But I have promises to keep."

Indent five spaces from the left margin and double-space prose passages of more than four lines, and do not use quotation marks. Shorter passages may be written into your text.

Quotations within quotations

Use single quotations marks to enclose a direct quotation within a direct quotation.

The minister began his sermon: "In the Book of Genesis we read that 'In the beginning God created the heavens and the earth.'" [Notice that two sets of quotation marks appear after *earth*. The single quotation mark completes the internal quote and the double quotation mark completes the main quote.]

NOTE: On a typewriter a single quotation mark is made with the apostrophe key.

Titles

Use quotation marks around the titles of shorter works such as songs, short stories, articles, poems, and essays.

Archie read Robert Browning's "My Last Duchess" and Edgar Allen Poe's "The Cask of Amontillado."

Words used in special or ironical senses

Use quotation marks or italics when a word is used as a word and not for its dictionary meaning.

"Relevant" and "receipt" are difficult words for Ann to spell.

Quotation marks may be used to enclose a word used ironically. For effectiveness, however, this device should be used sparingly.

The mother of the maimed child was not pleased with the "justice" of the judge's verdict. [ironic sense of the word "justice"]

NOTE: You should not use quotation marks to set off a slang term.

Quotation marks used with other marks of punctuation

This is a troublesome issue for many writers. It is wise to remember the following rules.

Periods and commas are always placed inside the closing quotation marks.

He read *Catcher in the Rye,* "The Fall of the House of Usher," and "Mending Wall."

Semicolons and colons are always placed outside of quotation marks.

Jonathan Kozol said that we should "Launch an all-out national attack on illiteracy"; he went on to say, "We should start this battle in a non-school setting."

Question marks, exclamation points, and dashes may be placed inside or outside the closing quotation marks. They are placed inside the quotation marks when they are part of the quote and outside when they are not.

My father asked, "Will you arrive before the end of July?"
Was it Franklin who said, "Hitch your wagon to a star"?

For additional information about quotation marks see the following sections:

Italics, (**ital**), p. 85
Uses of Brackets, ([]), p. 116
Uses of the Ellipsis Mark and the Slash, (**p/. . .**), (**p//**), p. 124

EXERCISE

Insert quotation marks as needed in the following sentences. Use C to designate a correct sentence.

1. Speaker O'Neill said I used to be the lone voice crying out there.
2. Speaker O'Neill said that he used to be the lone voice crying out there.
3. Why is he screaming is she hurt asked the lifeguard?
4. He asked the piano player if he would play Jude and Stardust.

5. Try to add variety to your sentence structure the teacher suggested.
6. If she says shut up once more I'll leave exclaimed Stephanie.
7. Jamie said I'm hungry.
8. E. E. Cummings used the pronouns anyone and someone in an unusual way in his poem anyone lived in a pretty how town, explained the critic.
9. Did you hear him say, 'I'll get even with you?' asked the judge.
10. Joel said that he was tired.

29
USES OF THE APOSTROPHE   p/'

Although the apostrophe fits into this section neatly, it is not really a punctuation mark. The other marks of punctuation clarify sentence structure. The apostrophe clarifies word form. The apostrophe is used primarily to show the possessive case of nouns and some pronouns, to mark the omission of letters in contracted words and numbers, and to indicate the plural of letters and numbers. The apostrophe is used in the situations discussed below.

Possessive case forms

An apostrophe is used with the singular and plural forms of nouns that do not end in *s* and with indefinite pronouns to show possession.

> Reagan's economy
> Hawkeye's surgical instruments
> everybody's problem
> the woman's clothing
> the women's clothing

> NOTE: Do not use an apostrophe with personal pronouns.
>
> his books
> its parks

> NOTE: The possessive case of many nouns is formed with *of* (foot of the stairs, leg of the table). As a general rule, avoid using

an apostrophe *s* with inanimate objects. Although the *of* form is acceptable with animate objects, the apostrophe is more generally accepted.

> the dog's bark [common]
> the bark of the dog [less common]
> the mouth of the river [common]
> the river's mouth [less common]

When a singular noun ends in *s,* form the possessive with an apostrophe followed by an *s* if the *s* is pronounced as an extra syllable.

> waitress's uniform
> Jones's butcher shop

Use only an apostrophe if the word is difficult to pronounce with the extra syllable.

> Aristophanes' plays
> Jesus' teachings

When the plural of a noun ends in *s,* add just the apostrophe after the *s* to show possession.

> the girls' basketball team
> the Joneses' canoes

When two or more nouns show individual possession, use an apostrophe with each.

> Jane Austen's and Emily Brontë's novels are still read in many high schools.

Add the apostrophe only to the second word of a pair if the pair shows joint possession.

> Dick and Virginia's apartment is newly furnished.

In compound nouns and relationship words add the apostrophe only to the last word.

> mother-in-law's book
> budget director's decision

29 / Exercise

Contractions

Use the apostrophe to indicate the omission of one or more letters to form contractions. Contractions represent spoken language. They are appropriate in most informal writing.

Formal	Informal
cannot	can't
do not	don't
it is	it's

Plurals of letters and numbers

An apostrophe before an *s* is used to form the plural of numbers, letters, figures, and words named as words.

There are three five's in my license plate.

I'll have two size 9's.

The frequent use of *and's* and *but's* suggests that the author relies heavily on compound constructions.

the early 1700's

NOTE: In dates, either *1700's* or *1700s* is acceptable as long as usage is consistent.

For further discussion of related topics, see the following:

Part 2, Personal pronouns, p. 21
Part 2, Possessive case, p. 21
Spelling, (**sp,**) p. 147

EXERCISE

Add apostrophes where they are needed in the sentences below.

1. The 1920s is a decade known for its carefree style of life.
2. Isnt "Fern Hill" Dylan Thomas poem?
3. My mother-in-laws telephone number has two 6s and three 3s.
4. Its nearly nine oclock, and the bark of the dog can be heard in the distance.

5. Sophocles tragedies demonstrate Aristotles concept of the tragic hero.
6. They borrowed their father-in-laws *Trivial Pursuit* game, and theyre still playing it three days later.
7. The mens store was across the street from the womens.
8. Shakespeares character, Hamlet, continues to challenge actors.
9. Charles class schedule was changed three times.
10. Carpenters salaries have decreased in the last two years.

30
USES OF THE ELLIPSIS MARK AND THE SLASH

Ellipsis mark

Use the ellipsis mark to show an omission from quoted material. The ellipsis mark consists of three spaced periods (. . .). When an ellipsis mark follows a sentence, it appears as four periods (. . . .) — one period ends the sentence and the other three signal the omission.

The two paragraphs below illustrate how the ellipsis mark can be used.

> On the morning of June 12, 1497, Elizabeth of York hurried with her five-year-old son Henry from her mother-in-law's house Coldharbour in Thames Street to the Tower of London. Reaching the Outer Ward they entered the White Tower through Coldharbour Gate, then climbed as rapidly as they could the flight of steps that led to the entrance of the great keep. Here, within the massive walls of William the Conqueror's strong fortress, they would be safe.
> — Carolly Erickson

Now observe the two uses of the ellipsis mark below:

> On the morning of June 12, 1497, Elizabeth of York hurried . . . from her mother-in-law's house Coldharbour in Thames Street to the Tower of London. Reaching the Outer Ward they entered the White Tower through Coldharbour Gate, then climbed as rapidly as they could the flight of steps that

led to the entrance of the great keep. . . . Here they would be safe. [The first omission (. . .) is from the middle of a sentence; the second (. . . .) occurs at the end of a sentence and includes a period.]

Slash

Use the slash to separate two lines of poetry that are written into the text. (Three or more lines of poetry should be set off by indenting five spaces from the left margin and single-spacing.)

Wordsworth concludes his "Lines (Composed a Few Miles Above Tintern Abbey)" by asserting, "And this green pastoral landscape, were to me/More dear, both for themselves and for thy sake."

Use a slash to indicate options.

pass/fail grading system

Many interest groups accuse television of exploiting sex and/or violence.

NOTE: The *and/or* construction should be used sparingly. Avoid using such constructions as *he/she* and *s/he*.

EXERCISE: PUNCTUATION REVIEW

Review all of the punctuation rules in Sections 20–30 before completing this exercise.

Explain the punctuation in the following five sentences by stating which punctuation rule(s) is followed in each.

1. There is always a temptation to think that the issues of one's own time are somehow special — maybe unique.
 — Randolph Quirk
2. "We are all in the gutter, but some of us are looking at the stars," wrote Oscar Wilde. . . . The same applies to language: we all make mistakes (somebody just wrote me to point out a badly constructed sentence in one of my columns), but some of us at least try to maintain standards.
 — John Simon

3. Within the present century, we have seen English (and virtually all other langauges) responding . . . to the mental technology of Freud.

— Randolph Quirk

4. At the beginning of *Macbeth,* a bleeding sergeant describes how brave Macbeth killed the "merciless" rebel, MacDonwald: "he unseamed him from the jaw to th' chops," that is, from the navel to the jaw, "and fixed his head upon our battlements."

— Robert Burchfield

5. I was told before arriving that I would probably be a "sight" for the village: I took this to mean that people of my complexion were rarely seen in Switzerland, and also that city people are always something of a "sight" outside of the city.

— James Baldwin

Punctuate the following sentences. Use C to designate a correct sentence.

1. Do you ever go skiing on weekends he asked.
2. He yelled help I'm falling.
3. Amy never dots her is or crosses her ts.
4. Miss Jones who is quite old has been a teacher for twenty-eight years.
5. Did you hear him say I'll get even with her asked Gerry.
6. The Roaring Twenties the colorful decade of the 1920s in the United States had other nicknames including the Dollar Decade and the Jazz Age.
7. During World War I 1914–1918 many Americans responded to President Woodrow Wilson's call to make the world safe for democracy.
8. In the 1920's people wanted to forget about World War I by amusing themselves with stock profits illegal liquor and new dances.
9. Have you read Browning's My Last Duchess.
10. Freds mother in law Mrs. Whitstone said that Fred had not been home for two days.

31
PARAGRAPHS ¶, no ¶

Writers use paragraphs to organize sentences into larger units of thought and to alert readers to a shift in focus. Like an essay, the paragraph should be coherent, developed, and unified. Most student paragraphs should contain a topic sentence and enough facts and examples to satisfy the reader that the topic has been adequately developed. Occasionally, however, a paragraph may be as short as one sentence. These short paragraphs often serve as transitional paragraphs joining one paragraph to another. The following paragraph is an example of a transitional paragraph.

> Now that we have examined the reasons for requiring handgun registration, let's look at some reasons for not registering handguns.

The first line of each new paragraph is indented from the left-hand margin (five spaces if you type your papers).

The two most common errors in paragraph division are not paragraphing enough and paragraphing too much. When these problems occur, the proofreader's mark, ¶, is used when you need to begin another paragraph, and, no ¶, when you unnecessarily begin a new paragraph.

Sections 32–35 of this part include brief discussions of the most common problems that confront writers as they compose paragraphs: unity, coherence, development, and introductory and concluding paragraphs. You should study these sections and do the exercises that accompany them if you are having difficulty with paragraphing.

32
PARAGRAPH UNITY ¶ un

Most paragraphs should contain a topic sentence that clearly announces what the paragraph is about. The topic sentence is generally the first sentence of a paragraph (or the second, following a transitional sentence), but it may occasionally be placed at the end of the paragraph to vary paragraph structure and to add a dramatic effect.

¶ un   128   An Alphabetical List of Frequent Writing Problems

Sometimes the main idea of a paragraph is so obvious that it does not need to be stated directly. Most of your paragraphs, however, should have the topic sentence as the first sentence, and each sentence that follows should stick to the topic and not discuss irrelevant issues. As you proofread your paper, ask yourself how each sentence relates to the central idea. If you can't explain the relationship, discard the idea and compose another sentence that shows a clearer relationship.

In the paragraph below notice how the first sentence establishes a situation and the rest of the paragraph develops or tells what happened as a result of that situation.

Somehow or other in my later years at Berkeley, two professors, Moses and Howison, representing opposite schools of thought, got into a controversy, probably about their classes. They brought together in the house of one of them a few of their picked students, with the evident intention of letting us show in conversation how much or how little we had understood of their respective teachings. I don't remember just what the subject was that they threw into the ring, but we wrestled with it till the professors could stand it no longer. Then they broke in, and while we sat silent and highly entertained, they went at each other hard and fast and long. It was after midnight when, the debate over, we went home. I asked the other fellows what they had got out of it, and their answers showed that they had seen nothing but a fine, fair fight. When I laughed, they asked me what I, the D.S., had seen that was so much more profound.

— Lincoln Steffens

Now observe the lack of unity in the student paragraph below.

```
One significant difference between scuba
diving and snorkeling is cost.  Scuba diving is an
expensive sport.  The initial investment is pro-
hibitive for most people.  If you don't own your
own equipment, you must rent air tanks, fins,
```

mask, wet suit, and weight belt. The only gear you use when you snorkel is a snorkel, mask, and fins. Snorkeling doesn't require much training because the equipment is easy to use. Snorkeling is often done in shallow water that is close to shore. Scuba diving, however, is often done off the side of a boat in deep water.

In the topic sentence, although the student promised to discuss the difference in cost between scuba diving and snorkeling, she did not deliver on her promise with supporting details. She discussed cost in sentences two, three, and four, but she didn't develop the topic. In sentence five she drifts away from discussing cost to training; and in sentences six and seven, to discussing water depth.

This writer has two choices to unify this paragraph. She could broaden the topic sentence so that the information in sentences five, six, and seven is relevant; or she could eliminate the unrelated sentences and further develop the topic of cost. The second choice offers more hope for a unified and well-developed paragraph because it establishes a clearer focus in the topic sentence. Notice how the revised version that follows develops only the notion of cost.

The excessive cost of scuba diving is what makes snorkeling a much wiser choice for the inexperienced diver. It is difficult for an aspiring scuba diver to get his fins wet for less than four hundred dollars. Likewise, the rental fee for air tanks, fins, mask, wet suit, and weight belt is prohibitive. Snorkeling, on the other hand, requires only a snorkel, mask, and fins. For less than a hundred dollars, a budding diver can be equipped like the pros.

EXERCISE

Comment on the use of unity in the following two paragraphs.

1. He came some minutes before eight. He was in his late twenties, small and carefully dressed, handsome, with a well-barbered head of hair. I didn't like him. I saw him as a man of simple origins, simply educated, but with a great sneering pride, deferential but resentful, not liking himself for what he was doing. He was the kind of man who, without political doctrine, only with resentments, had made the Iranian revolution. It would have been interesting to talk to him for an hour or two; it was going to be hard to be with him for some days, as I had now engaged myself to be.
   — V. S. Naipaul
2. Scott's novels suggested desirable standards, not just for young gentlemen but for gentlemen of all ages. Moreover, his influence was extended by example as well as by his novels. Perhaps the most influential and successful character created by him was himself. Most people assume one or more roles at some stage in their lives, with varying degrees of success; novelists, not surprisingly, tend to be especially good at doing so. Scott's role was completely successful, because he believed in it. Failing the profession of a soldier, which was barred to him, he thought that there was no better life than that of a Scottish laird living on his estates; and that is what he became. He bought the property which he renamed Abbotsford in 1811. He started with a cottage and a small farm, but by the 1820's he was Sir Walter Scott, Bart., owner of a full-blown country house on an estate of fourteen hundred acres.
   — Mark Girouard

33
PARAGRAPH COHERENCE ¶ coh

Good writing must be coherent; it should move from beginning to end according to a logical plan. In a paragraph, coherence means that the sentences are logically connected. A paragraph should not be a sequence of isolated sentences that the reader must link together. Rather, make certain that your sentences flow smoothly into one another. In short, make your point smoothly and clearly in each paragraph.

Obviously, your first step in achieving paragraph coherence is to follow a clear order such as *time, space,* or *logic. Time order* moves from beginning to end as in explaining a process or telling what happened. *Space order* moves from right to left, top to bottom, or near to far as in a description of a place. *Logical order* moves from cause to effect, particular to general, or comparison of *A* with *B*. The topic sentence is often the key to coherence because it helps to assure that subsequent sentences will follow logically.

Unfortunately, sentences are not always automatically linked just because they follow one another in a clear order. Consequently, writers often achieve paragraph coherence by using the following devices:

1. Repeated key words and phrases
2. Transitional words and phrases
3. Pronoun reference
4. Conjunctive adverbs (words that connect thought such as *moreover, consequently,* and *therefore*)
5. Demonstrative adjectives (words that "point" such as *this* sentence, *that* idea)
6. Parallel structure

Notice how coherence is achieved in the paragraph below. (The devices that the author uses for coherence are italicized.)

> The most persistent disputes between Eden and Churchill, apart from DeGaulle, concerned relations with Soviet Russia. After Hitler's attack on Russia, *Eden* was strongly pro-Soviet at the start and cooled off later; *Churchill* was cautious in

the early days and became enthusiastic later. *Their first dispute* came over the Soviet demand, made even when the Germans were at the gates of Moscow, that the Western powers should recognize unconditionally the Soviet frontiers of 1941. *Eden* was for agreeing, *Churchill* against. *Curiously,* Molotov finally stilled the argument by agreeing to an Anglo-Soviet alliance without any mention of frontiers. *In the end* it was Churchill at Yalta who agreed to the Soviet demand.
— A. J. P. Taylor

3

4, 5

6

This paragraph is coherent largely because of the control of the topic sentence. This opening sentence announces that the paragraph will discuss the disputes of Eden and Churchill over Soviet Russia. The second sentence is syntactically balanced, and the names *Eden* and *Churchill* are repeated in their respective halves of the sentence. The phrase *their first dispute* clearly links sentence three to the topic sentence. Sentence four is balanced syntactically, and the names *Eden* and *Churchill* are repeated in parallel structure. In sentence five, *curiously* functions conjunctively by joining it to the previous four sentences. Sentence six brings the paragraph to a logical conclusion with the phrase *in the end*.

As you read the student paragraph that follows, try to identify what is wrong with the use of coherence.

Mark Quigley is the biggest boy in our class. He is the center on the basketball team. He is a poor sport on the court. He constantly fouls players who are smaller. He broke the ribs of a guard on the opposing team last week. Mark punched another player just because he could jump higher. If another team has a taller center, he becomes docile and rarely commits a foul.

This paragraph certainly has unity, but you should recognize that something is not right. The paragraph is choppy. Although the sentences all relate to Mark Quigley, they are not joined together smoothly. In short, the paragraph is not coherent. Notice that the paragraph below is much more coherent. (The devices used for coherence are italicized.)

Mark Quigley, the biggest boy in our class, is the center on the basketball team. *Because of his size,* he often is a poor sport on the court, and he constantly fouls players who are smaller. *Last week* he broke the ribs of a guard on the opposing team. *In the next game* Mark punched another player just because he could jump higher. *Like many poor sports,* Mark becomes docile and rarely commits a foul if the other team has a larger player.

EXERCISE

Explain how coherence is achieved in the following paragraphs:

1. There are three main counts to the indictment, listed at the outset of the report. First, increased government regulation, which has increased production costs. Second, high taxes, which have reduced incentives to work and save. Third, transfer payments for welfare and social security, which have reduced "employment of the poor and of older workers."

— Emma Rothschild

2. They live up alongside the hills, in hollow after hollow. They live in eastern Kentucky and eastern Tennessee and in the western part of North Carolina and the western part of Virginia and in just about the whole state of West Virginia. They live close to the land; they farm it and some of them go down into it to extract its coal. Their ancestors, a century or two ago, fought their way westward from the Atlantic seaboard, came up on the mountains, penetrated the valleys, and moved stubbornly up the creeks for room, for privacy, for a view, for a domain of sorts. They are Appalachian people, mountain people, hill people. They are white yeomen, or miners, or hollow folk, or subsistence farmers.

— Robert Coles

34
PARAGRAPH DEVELOPMENT ¶ dev

A paragraph that is adequately developed is one that presents sufficient details, examples, and illustrations to support the topic sentence. The topic sentence is a generalization about a topic, and it is generally the first sentence in a paragraph. A diagram of a typical paragraph of expository writing would look like this:

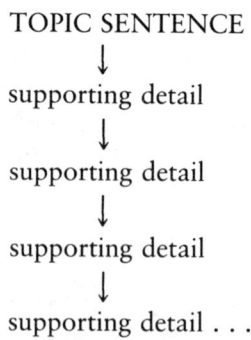

How much supporting detail is needed for adequate development is relative. Each paragraph must be judged independently, and the amount and method of development are often determined by the scope of the topic sentence. A paragraph that is inadequately developed burdens the reader with a useless generalization. Short paragraphs of one or two sentences are usually employed only for transition or emphasis. The paragraph below is not adequately developed. (The topic sentence is italicized.)

> Now it is a historical truism that many immigrants, and not a few other Americans, have faced discrimination. *But history also shows that the main reason was their own poverty and powerlessness, and other people's ethnic or racial prejudice; the kind of English they spoke, or whether they spoke it at all, have little if anything to do with the matter.*

As interesting as the above paragraph is, it is not completely developed. The topic sentence is clear, but the reader is left with a generalization. We want to hear about the specific examples that demonstrate that people are not discriminated against because of the English they speak. Notice the detail that the author Robert Claiborne adds in the complete version of this paragraph. (The topic sentence is italicized.)

> Now it is a historical truism that many immigrants, and not a few other Americans, have faced discrimination. *But history also shows that the main reason was their own poverty and powerlessness, and other people's ethnic or racial*

prejudice; the kind of English they spoke, or whether they spoke it at all, have little if anything to do with the matter. Irish immigrants, nearly all of whom spoke English, were early targets of discrimination; so were their children, even those who learned to "manipulate" American upper-class dialects. Immigrant Jews, whose English was almost invariably accented, were discriminated against, but so were their children, speaking English from birth, who prior to World War II were admitted to most private colleges only in small numbers, and were flatly excluded from some jobs and "restricted" neighborhoods. And American blacks still face widespread discrimination, whether their English is Black English or Ivy League. Indeed there have been periods in our history when an educated black, speaking standard English, was considered an "uppity nigger" requiring special treatment; readers who know their *Huckleberry Finn* will recall old Finn's drunken rage at encountering a well-dressed, well-spoken black "college p'fessor" who could "talk all kinds of languages and knowed everything."

— Robert Claiborne

Claiborne's paragraph from *Our Marvelous Native Tongue: The Life and Times of the English Language,* though long, is thoroughly developed with examples and illustrations. This is a common method of paragraph development. Sometimes, however, you may use a different method to present your details, examples, and illustrations. Here is a list of some of the most common ways to develop paragraphs. (Frequently more than one of the methods will be used to develop a single paragraph.)

1. *Illustration* — The writer presents facts or illustrations that support the general topic.
2. *Definition* — The writer must make clear what the term means and what it does not mean.
3. *Comparison and contrast* — The writer must be certain that the items to be compared/contrasted belong to the same class. (Analogy is a type of comparison that uses something familiar to the reader to illuminate something unfamiliar.)

4. *Cause and effect* — The writer usually investigates the reason or the consequences for something.
5. *Classification* — The writer discusses something according to its constituent parts.

EXERCISE

Discuss the development of the paragraph below. Be prepared to discuss topic sentences and methods of development.

1. Let us define a plot. We have defined a story as a narrative of events arranged in their time sequence. A plot is also a narrative of events, the emphasis falling on causality. "The king died and then the queen died" is a story. "The king died and then the queen died of grief" is a plot. The time sequence is preserved, but the sense of causality overshadows it. Or again: "The queen died, no one knew why, until it was discovered that it was through grief at the death of the king." This is a plot with a mystery in it, a form capable of high development. It suspends the time sequence, it moves as far away from the story as its limitations will allow. Consider the death of the queen. If it is in a story we say, "and then?" If it is in a plot we ask "Why?" That is the fundamental difference between the two aspects of a novel. A plot cannot be told to a gaping audience of cavemen or to a tyrannical sultan or to their modern descendants the movie-public. They can only be kept awake by "and then — and then — ." They can only supply curiosity. But a plot demands intelligence and memory also.
— E. M. Forster
2. For many regulars, Friday night at the coliseum is the major social event of the week. All over the arena blacks, browns, and whites visit easily across ethnic lines, in perverse defiance of stereotypes about blue-collar prejudices. A lot of people in the ringside section know each other, by sight if not by name. Mrs. Elizabeth Chappell, better known simply as "Mama," has been coming to the matches for more than twenty-five years. Between bouts, she walks around the ring, visiting with old friends and making new ones. When she beats on a fallen villain with a huge mallet she carries in a shopping bag, folks shout, "Attaway, Mama! Get him!" and agree that "things don't really

start to pick up till Mama gets here." When a dapper young insurance salesman flies into a rage at a referee's decision, the fans nudge one another and grin about how "old Freddy really gets worked up, don't he?"

— William C. Martin

3. Thoreau's assault on the Concord society of the mid-nineteenth century has the quality of a modern Western: he rides into the subject at top speed, shooting in all directions. Many of his shots ricochet and nick him on the rebound, and throughout the melee there is a horrendous cloud of inconsistencies and contradictions, and when the shouting dies down and the air clears, one is impressed chiefly by the courage of the rider and by how splendid it was that somebody should have ridden in there and raised all that ruckus.

— E. B. White

35
INTRODUCTORY AND CONCLUDING PARAGRAPHS

The introductory paragraph should incite your reader's interest and the concluding paragraph should satisfy it. An introductory paragraph is the first impression that a writer makes upon his readers, and for that reason alone it is important. An introductory paragraph should perform at least two tasks: (1) it should catch the attention of the reader and make him want to read further, and (2) it should announce what the essay is going to be about. Frequently the thesis sentence appears in the introductory paragraph (see Thesis Sentences, p. 158).

In the following paragraph, the intriguing opening sentence, an emphasis of the obvious, draws the reader to the thesis which tells what the writer plans to do — discuss what a college education should do to a student. The paragraph also suggests how the essay will be developed by stating that two personal experiences will be used as illustrations.

It is possible to get an education at a university. It has been done; not often, but the fact that a proportion, however small, of college students do get a start in interested, methodical study, proves my thesis, and the two personal experiences I have to illustrate it show how to circumvent the faculty, the other students, and the whole college system of mind-fixing. My method might lose a boy his degree, but a degree is not worth so much as the capacity and the drive to learn, and the undergraduate desire for any empty baccalaureate is one of the holds the educational system has on students. Wise students some day will refuse to take degrees, as the best men (in England, for instance) give, but do not themselves accept, titles.

— Lincoln Steffens

Among the most effective means for catching the interest of your readers are the following:

a direct quotation
an anecdote
a question
an interesting fact or statistic
an unusual statement

The following opening paragraph of an essay on aging effectively uses an anecdote.

There is an old American folk tale about a wooden bowl. It seems that Grandmother, with her trembling hands, was guilty of occasionally breaking a dish. Her daughter angrily gave her a wooden bowl, and told her that she must eat out of it from now on. The young granddaughter, observing this, asked her mother why Grandmother must eat from a wooden bowl when the rest of the family was given china plates. "Because she is old!" answered her mother. The child thought for a moment and then told her mother, "You must save the wooden bowl when Grandma dies." Her mother asked why, and the child replied, "For when you are old."

— Sharon R. Curtin

Concluding paragraphs should sum up the major points that have been presented in the essay. They also should bring the essay full circle by referring to something that was mentioned in the opening paragraph. This gives the reader the sense that you have completed your thought. You should never introduce new evidence in the concluding paragraph as it detracts from a sense of completeness. As with the introductory paragraph, an appropriate conclusion may be a direct quotation, an anecdote, a question, or an unusual statement that draws your thoughts to a close. In shorter essays like the ones you will probably write in your college writing classes, a closing may be a final sentence or two rather than a complete paragraph.

A good concluding statement usually reminds the reader of the main point of the paper, but it should not simply repeat the main point. Often the concluding statement will restate the thesis with a new emphasis. Essays may also end by asking a question that challenges the reader or, perhaps, with an anecdote. The conclusion should clearly show that the writer has finished and not just stopped. Notice how the following concluding paragraph gives such a sense of completeness. (The introductory paragraph of Virginia Woolf's essay is the first paragraph in the exercise below.)

> That is true: to escape is the greatest of pleasures; street haunting in winter the greatest of adventures. Still as we approach our own doorstep again, it is comforting to feel the old possessions, the old prejudices, fold us round; and the self, which has been blown about at so many street corners, which has been battered like a moth at the flame of so many inaccessible lanterns, sheltered and enclosed. Here again is the usual door; here the chair turned as we left it and the china bowl and the brown ring on the carpet. And here — let us examine it tenderly, let us touch it with reverence — is the only spoil we have retrieved from all the treasures of the city, a lead pencil.
>
> — Virginia Woolf

EXERCISE

Write an introductory paragraph on one of the following topics. Begin with something that will catch the attention of your readers. State your topic and your attitude toward your topic. Also, try to suggest how you plan to develop the essay.

1. The popularity of a spectator sport
2. Television commercials
3. Sexual freedom

Discuss the effectiveness of the following opening paragraphs:
1. No one perhaps has ever felt passionately towards a lead pencil. But there are circumstances in which it can become supremely desirable to possess one; moments when we are set upon having an object, an excuse for walking half across London between tea and dinner. As the fox hunter hunts in order to preserve the breed of foxes, and the golfer plays in order that open spaces may be preserved from the builders, so when the desire comes upon us to go street rambling a pencil does for a pretext, and getting up we say: "Really I must buy a pencil," as if under cover of this excuse we could indulge safely in the greatest pleasure of town life in winter — rambling the streets of London.
— Virginia Woolf
2. Lust is not interested in its partners, but only in the gratification of its own craving: not even in the satisfaction of our whole natures, but in the appeasement merely of an appetite which we are unable to subdue. It is therefore a form of self-subjection; in fact of self-emptying. The sign it wears is: "This property is vacant." Anyone may take possession of it for a while. Lustful people may think that they can choose a partner at will for sexual gratification. But they do not really choose; they accept what is available. Lust accepts any partner for a momentary service; anyone may squat in its groin.
— Henry Fairlie

36
INEFFECTIVE USE OF THE PASSIVE VOICE pas

Writers often have the option of putting transitive verbs in the active or the passive voice. Although the passive voice is grammatical, it is often not the best choice.

A sentence in the active voice reveals that the subject does the action.

Ronald Reagan   won   the election.
[noun phrase 1   +   verb   +   noun phrase 2]

In the passive voice the subject receives the action and is acted upon by an agent that may or may not be included in the

36 / Ineffective Use of the Passive Voice

construction, and therefore its use should be limited to specific situations where the writer wants to indicate passivity.

> The election   was   won   by Ronald Reagan.
> [noun phrase 2 + to be + verb + preposition and noun phrase 1]

Several changes take place in using the passive voice:

1. The doer of the action of the active sentence becomes the object of the preposition *by*.
2. The object of the active sentence becomes the subject of the passive sentence.
3. A form of *to be* appears before the main verb.

The use of the passive voice, then, becomes an issue of style. Passive constructions are weak and less direct than active sentences. They are more evasive and more wordy — at least two additional words are used in the passive voice. In general, the active voice is more precise and more vigorous.

The sentence below is evasive because it postpones (and possibly eliminates) the agent.

> It has been decided that your petition will not be accepted (by the school board).

The following sentence, in the active voice, is more vigorous and less cumbersome.

> The school board has decided not to accept your petition.

The passive voice should be used in the following situations.

If the agent or doer of the action is unknown, use the passive voice. In these situations the doer (subject) is not known and cannot be the subject of an active sentence.

> A building was torched in last night's riot.
> The family suspected that their camping trailer had been vandalized. [In this example the "that clause" is passive because the doer is unknown.]

When it is more important to emphasize the receiver of the action rather than the doer, use the passive voice.

John F. Kennedy was assassinated in Dallas, Texas, on November 22, 1963.

A gold Rolls Royce was driven in the parade.

EXERCISE

Identify whether the following sentences are in the active or the passive voice. If the sentence is in the passive voice, change it to active and decide which is a more effective sentence.

1. The fact has been widely acknowledged that the Republican Party is growing.
2. In Greek legend the elements of nature were represented by giants.
3. Edward Gibbon wrote the *History of the Decline and Fall of the Roman Empire*.
4. Care must be taken by writers when they use the passive voice.
5. Gloria Steinem founded *Ms.* magazine and the Women's Action Alliance.

37
ERRORS IN THE USE OF PRONOUNS: REFERENCE AND AGREEMENT

Agreement of pronouns

Each pronoun should agree with its antecedent in person and number. The antecedent is the word that a pronoun refers to.

Mark has always been a well-behaved child. He even offers to help his father clean the garage. [*He* is the third person singular masculine pronoun. It refers to and agrees with *Mark*, its antecedent.]

Writers frequently have problems with agreement between pronoun and antecedent in the situations described below.

Singular antecedents

When singular antecedents are joined by *and*, they take a plural pronoun whether the antecedents are singular or plural.

37 / Errors in the Use of Pronouns

The *president* and the *speaker* of the house could not agree on *their* assessment of the economy.

There are exceptions to this rule. When the two antecedents refer to a single idea, the pronoun is singular.

Ham and eggs — *it* is what I like best for breakfast.

When the compound antecedent is preceded by each or every, the pronoun should be singular.

Each student and faculty member should take *his* seat so the conference may begin.

Each student and faculty member should take *a* seat so the conference may begin.

Some writers prefer to use the pronoun *their* because it includes *his* and *her*. Although this is acceptable in informal writing, you should consult with your instructor before using this device. It is probably most desirable to change both the pronoun and antecedent to plural whenever possible. (The author does not like to accept the plural *their* with the singular antecedents *each* and *every*.)

All students and *faculty members* should take *their* seats so the conference may begin.

It is unfortunate that the English language does not have a singular pronoun that can stand for *his* and *her*. Constructions like *his/her* and *his or her* are cumbersome and should be avoided. Generally the consistent use of *their* is preferable to these constructions.

When the parts of a compound antecedent are joined with *or* or *nor*, the pronoun should agree with the nearer antecedent.

Neither the President nor the cabinet members could explain their defense policy.

Either David or Roderick left his wallet on the table.

Agreement of indefinite pronouns

Indefinite pronouns are always followed by singular pronouns. The most common indefinite pronouns are *each, every, either, anybody, somebody, anyone, someone, everyone* and *neither.*

Each of the ladies left little doubt about *her* opinion.

Every member of the field hockey team had *her* own locker.

When a singular subject is followed by a prepositional phrase with a plural object, the pronoun must agree with the subject of the sentence.

Each of the students carried *his* own books.

EXERCISE

Revise the following sentences so that pronouns and antecedents agree. Use C to designate a correct sentence.

1. Neither the coach nor his assistants could explain his behavior.
2. Each member was asked their opinion on the first motion.
3. Every mother thought that her child was the most talented.
4. Did anyone leave his glasses in the top drawer?
5. Either John or his parents lost the keys to his car.

Reference of pronouns

Pronouns do not have meaning themselves but derive their meaning from the nouns for which they substitute. Each pronoun must refer clearly to the noun for which it is substituted. Pronouns must agree with their antecedent in person and number.

FAULTY

In the second chapter it said that Richard I was the Black Knight in *Ivanhoe*. [There is no clear reference for *it*.]

CORRECT

The second chapter pointed out that Richard I was the Black Knight in *Ivanhoe*.

Writers often experience problems with pronoun reference in the following situations.

A pronoun must be placed as close as possible to its antecedent.

37 / Errors in the Use of Pronouns

Faulty

Bill went on a starvation diet and, as a result, he became tired and weak; but he did lose twenty pounds. It was not good for his health. [The reference for *it* is remote.]

Correct

Bill went on a starvation diet and, as a result, he became tired and weak; but he did lose twenty pounds. The diet, however, was not good for his health.

A pronoun must refer to only one antecedent.

Faulty

Matt's father told my brother that *he* would leave tomorrow. [Does *he* refer to the father or the brother?]

Correct

Matt's father said to my brother, "I will leave tomorrow."

A pronoun should not refer to an implied antecedent. *It, this, who,* and *which* are especially troublesome. Do not use a pronoun to refer to a whole idea.

Faulty

John and Sally spent last weekend with a marriage counselor. That has helped them. [*That* is a broad and ambiguous reference.]

Correct

John and Sally were helped by the weekend that they spent with a marriage counselor.

Faulty

Interest charges often add thousands of dollars to the price of a house. This should be taken into consideration when budgeting for such a purchase. [*This* is not a clear reference.]

Correct

The fact that interest charges often add thousands of dollars to the price of a house should be taken into consideration when budgeting for such a purchase.

FAULTY
In the professor's lecture, he talked about economic determinism. [*He* has no clear antecedent.]

CORRECT
In his lecture the professor talked about economic determinism.

All papers should have titles, but a pronoun should not refer to the title in the opening sentence of an essay.

For example, if the title of your paper is "Buying a Used Car," don't begin with a sentence like "This is often risky because. . . ." Rather, begin with "Buying a used car is often risky because. . . ."

The use of *you* is permissible in informal writing as long as it refers directly to the reader. In formal writing, however, *one* should be used.

In Steve's high school *you* can choose elective courses.

In Steve's high school *one* can choose elective courses. [better]

In Steve's high school students can choose elective courses. [best]

NOTE: Try to avoid overusing the indefinite *you* in your writing. Overuse creates an awkward point of view that may alienate and frustrate your reader.

For further information about pronouns see the following section:

Part 2, Pronouns, pp. 21–22

EXERCISE

Revise the following sentences so that all of the pronouns refer clearly to their appropriate antecedents. Use C to designate a correct sentence.

1. The president told the vice-president that he should meet with the secretary of state.
2. As soon as Mrs. Thatcher broke the bottle over the bow of the submarine, she was set afloat in the North Sea.

38 / Spelling

3. On page 291 of the textbook, it said that orthography is the discipline of spelling.
4. The veterinarian wanted a deposit before he would perform surgery. This is common in many veterinarian clinics.
5. The United States and Israel established closer diplomatic ties. This greatly upset Egypt.
6. Three automobiles were stolen in Mrs. Robinson's neighborhood last month. This made all of the neighbors very apprehensive.
7. Marion has written several short stories, but she can't seem to get any of them published.
8. In the school newspaper they are always commenting on the student parking problem.
9. In Los Angeles you can dress any way you want to.
10. Molly has always been interested in chemistry, but she doesn't think she will major in it in college.

38
SPELLING   sp

English spelling presents problems for most writers because the spelling system is full of irregularities and contradictions. Nevertheless, correct spelling is essential, and misspelling makes a writer appear lazy and incompetent. Some writers naturally spell well, but many more struggle with poor spelling each time they write. If you are a poor speller, try using the suggestions that follow to improve your spelling skills.

Proofread

Spelling is closely related to proofreading. After you write your paper, allow yourself time to look up all words that you are in doubt about before you type your finished copy or before you submit your in-class paper. Use a good collegiate dictionary. Don't worry too much about the spelling on your first draft because this concern will only interfere with the continuity of your writing.

Develop special "tricks"

Develop your own special tricks. Devise rules for yourself, for example, the *er* in *letter* and *paper* can remind you that *statio-*

nery ends in *ery* rather than *ary*. *Their, there,* and *they're* all begin with *the*; and *believe* has the word *lie* in it. You can make up your own rules and have fun doing it.

Learn spelling rules

Although spelling rules are frequently more confusing than the memorization of individual words, there are some rules that can be very helpful.

Double the final consonant. In one-syllable words (*wrap*) ending in a single consonant (*p*) that is preceded by a single vowel (*a*), double the final consonant before an ending that begins with a vowel such as *-ing, -ed, -en, -er, -est, -y.*

fog	foggy
pad	padding
rot	rotted
fat	fattest

The same rule applies to two-syllable words that have the accent on the second syllable.

forgét	forgétting
begín	begínning

Do not double the final consonant in two-syllable words if the final syllable is not accented.

coúnsel	coúnseled
óffer	óffered

NOTE: Do not double the final consonant if the vowel is long or if the word ends in a silent *e*.

relate	related
beat	beaten
come	coming
dine	dining
hope	hoped

Drop the final *e*. Drop the unpronounced *e* (pleas*e*) before adding an ending that begins with a vowel (pleas*ed*, pleas*ing*).

desire   desired
endure   enduring
sure   surer

Retain the final *e* before suffixes that begin with consonants.

awe   awesome
hope   hopeful
care   careful
advertise advertisement

Change *y* to *i*. When adding a suffix to a word ending in *y*, change the *y* to *i* if it is preceded by a consonant.

fly   flies
ally   allies
try   tries

This rule does not apply with the suffix *ing*.

fly   flying
apply applying

If the *y* is preceded by a vowel, do not change *y* to *i*.

play   played
annoy annoyed

Follow the *i* before *e* rule. When the sound is *ee* as in *belief*, place *i* before *e* except after *c*.

i BEFORE *e*   EXCEPT AFTER *c*
belief   deceit
grief   conceive
thief   ceiling

In addition, if *e* sounds like *a* as in *neighbor* or *weight*, place *e* before *i*.

vein
freight
sleigh

sp | 150 An Alphabetical List of Frequent Writing Problems

Do not rely on pronunciation

To illustrate how distinct English spelling is from pronunciation, George Bernard Shaw once argued that the word *fish* could just as logically be spelled *ghoti*.

gh = f as in tou*gh*
o = i as in w*o*men
ti = sh as in mo*ti*on

This is an extreme example, but it makes a very important point about spelling.

Pronunciation is a particularly unreliable guide with homonyms — words pronounced the same that have different spellings and meanings such as *fair* and *fare*, or *lead* and *led*. Study the following list of frequently confused words and learn the correct usage for each.

accept	except	
affect	effect (noun)	effect (verb)
all ready	already	
allusion	illusion	
born	borne	
brake	break	
breath	breathe	
canvas	canvass	
capital	capitol	
conscience	conscious	
desert	dessert	
forth	fourth	
lead (verb)	lead (noun)	led (verb)
maybe	may be	
patience	patients	
principal	principle	
to	too	two
vice	vise	
weather	whether	
weak	week	
your	you're	

38 / Spelling sp

Spelling errors often occur when words are mispronounced—usually giving them more or fewer syllables and sounds than they need.

Correct	Incorrect
athlete	athelete
February	Febuary
library	libary
medieval	medeval

Make a list

When you look up a word that you are in doubt about, jot it down on a personal list of misspelled words. Memorize how the word is spelled and force yourself to use it often. You can begin by studying the following list of fifty frequently misspelled words.

absence	efficient	preceding
accommodation	embarrass	prejudice
achievement	environment	privilege
adjustment	exaggeration	receive
analysis	exercise	relevant
anniversary	ghetto	repetition
argument	humorous	roommate
attendance	innocent	secretary
basically	irrelevant	similar
becoming	jeopardize	suspicious
beginning	laboratory	technique
column	manageable	thorough
committee	misspelled	truly
conscientious	nineteen	undoubtedly
correspondence	ninety	whether
counselor	occasionally	wholly
definitely	parallel	

Spelling of foreign plurals

Use your dictionary to find the plural of every noun that has irregular plurals. This is especially true with foreign nouns borrowed into English. Here is a list of some of the more frequent nouns that have a foreign plural.

Singular	Plural
alumnus	alumni
analysis	analyses
basis	bases
crisis	crises
criterion	criteria
curriculum	curricula (or *ums*)
datum	data
memorandum	memoranda
stimulus	stimuli
formula	formulae (*as*)
hypothesis	hypotheses
thesis	theses

Study the components of words

Be familiar with the root, prefix, and suffix of a word. If, for example, you see that the root of a word is *finite*, you are not likely to write *definate*. If you know that the prefix of a word is *super*, you are not likely to write *supravise*.

EXERCISE

Correct the one word that is misspelled in each of the following groups.

1. abcense, argument, competent
2. condemn, conciet, accommodate
3. adequatly, beginning, convenience
4. benefitted, coolly, copies
5. amatuer, column, disappear
6. appropriate, comission, disappoint
7. medieval, merely, hinderance
8. eithth, illiterate, incidentally
9. exceed, exaggerate, paralel
10. gauge, personnel, posess

11. reminise, succeed, practically
12. rythm, representative, syllable
13. privlege, schedule, procedure
14. professor, sergeant, truley
15. tyrany, psychology, siege

Write the plural form of the following nouns.

1. ally
2. thesis
3. laundry
4. hypothesis
5. tragedy
6. reply
7. democracy
8. turkey
9. datum
10. baby
11. treaty
12. navy
13. puppy
14. comedy

39
FAULTY SUBORDINATION sub

Two or more independent clauses (simple sentences) can be joined by one of two processes: coordination and subordination. *Coordination* gives the two ideas equal grammatical emphasis. (You should study the section Faulty Coordination, p. 65, before continuing with this section.)

Subordination is a technique that indicates one idea is not as important as the other. Notice what happens to the emphasis in the following simple sentences:

TWO SENTENCES
Ronald Reagan was elected President of the United States. He was sixty-nine years old.

COORDINATION
Ronald Reagan was elected President of the United States, and he was sixty-nine years old.

SUBORDINATION (RELATIVE PRONOUN)
Ronald Reagan, *who* was sixty-nine years old, was elected President of the United States.

Subordination is the most logical choice in the above examples because it correctly emphasizes the main idea — Reagan's being elected — and places less emphasis on his age, which is of secondary importance. It is possible, however, that if one were writing about significant achievements of senior citizens, Reagan's age would be emphasized.

Ronald Reagan was sixty-nine years old when he was elected President of the United States.

Subordination is an important skill for writers to master. If it were not for subordination, your prose would sound childish and monotonous. Consider the excessive use of coordination in the following passage.

My sister spent last summer at Lake Tahoe. She worked as a waitress at Ron's. Ron's is a small luncheonette. She saved enough to pay for her tuition.

Now notice how using subordination in the following sentence eliminates the monotony of excessive coordination.

My sister, who spent last summer at Lake Tahoe working as a waitress at Ron's, a small luncheonette, saved enough to pay for her tuition.

Writers often have problems with faulty subordination in the following situations.

Choose the correct subordinating conjunction. Subordinating conjunctions express different relationships — cause-and-effect, contrast, time, and place to name a few. Frequently used subordinating conjunctions are listed below.

after	before	unless	whereas
although	if	until	
because	since	when	

39 / Faulty Subordination   **sub**

FAULTY

Because the movie was over, the group of senior citizens went out for pizza and beer. [This sentence suggests an illogical cause relationship with the use of *because*. A time relationship is more logical.]

REVISED

After the movie was over, the group of senior citizens went out for pizza and beer.

Subordinate the less important idea. When you connect two or more ideas with subordination, be sure to emphasize the main idea and subordinate less important ideas.

FAULTY

Jane's grades, which will determine whether she will continue at the university, should arrive in the mail today. [With the context as given, the writer does not wish to emphasize the fact that the grades will arrive with the mail today. Jane's status at the university is the point that should be emphasized.]

REVISED

Jane's grades, which should arrive in the mail today, will determine whether she will continue at the university.

Avoid excessive subordination. Try to avoid using too many subordinate constructions in a sentence because they tend to make it confusing and awkward.

FAULTY

The city of Edinburgh, which is historic, has a castle that sits high above the city which is located on the banks of the Firth of Forth.

REVISED

In historic Edinburgh, which is located on the banks of the Firth of Forth, a castle sits high above the city.

For a discussion of related topics see the following:

Part 2, Parts of Speech, pp. 19–31
Faulty Coordination, (**coord**), p. 65

t | 156   An Alphabetical List of Frequent Writing Problems

EXERCISE

Use a subordinating conjunction or relative pronoun to combine the sentences below.

1. The Amazon is the world's second longest river. It is the major river in South America.
2. The Amazon is 4,000 miles long. It is longer than the distance between New York and San Francisco.
3. Vincente Pinzon was a Spanish explorer. He was probably the first European to see the Amazon.
4. Francisco de Orellana, a Spaniard, led the first exploration of the Amazon River by a European. His group was attacked by female Indian warriors. The Spaniards named their attackers Amazons. Amazons were female warriors in Greek mythology.
5. The fierce piranha and the pirarucu live in the Amazon. The pirarucu is the largest freshwater fish in South America.

40
ERRORS IN VERB TENSE | t

The verb tense system in English is complex. It is remarkable that most native speakers of English correctly use such a complex system. (For a review of the verb tense system study the section on verbs, pp. 23–24.)

In summary, here are the basic tense forms in English for the regular verb *to play*.

PRESENT	PAST
I play	I played
FUTURE	PRESENT PERFECT
I will play	I have played
PAST PERFECT	FUTURE PERFECT
I had played	I will have played

Writers who have problems with verb tense should study and use the following suggestions.

Do not shift tense unnecessarily. A change in tense usually

40 / Errors in Verb Tense

signals a change in time. You must be careful not to transmit false signals by switching tenses unnecessarily.

As Jack walked down the deserted street, he was suddenly aware that a pack of large dogs *is* following him. [incorrect]

As Jack walked down the deserted street, he was suddenly aware that a pack of large dogs *was* following him. [correct]

Use perfect tenses to show completed action. The perfect tenses indicate that an action was completed before another action began.

I have jogged so I can eat a large meal at the banquet tonight. [The act of jogging is completed at the time of the statement — *present perfect.*]

Matthew had finished reviewing his paper when the teacher walked in the classroom. [Past action was completed before another past action — *past perfect.*]

The Secretary of Defense feels that he will have convinced the committee to support him before the future vote. [Future action before the future vote — *future perfect.*]

Be careful not to mix the perfect tenses. Present perfect must be used with present tense, past perfect with past tense, and future perfect with future tense.

Faulty

We had completed the first leg of the relay, and we are ready to begin the second. [Incorrect shift from past perfect to present tense.]

Revised

We had completed the first leg of the relay, and we were ready to begin the second. [past perfect with past tense]

Revised

We have completed the first leg of the relay, and we are ready to begin the second. [present perfect with present tense]

Use correct tense when writing about events in the past. When you are writing about events in the past, you may use either the past or present tense (this is called historical present), but you must stay with the tense that you choose. Always use the historical present when summarizing plots of literature and movies.

> John Reed rode with Pancho Villa during the Mexican Revolution, and he *develops* a sense of admiration for the peasant leader. [faulty shift from past to present]
>
> In *All Quiet on the Western Front* the protagonist learns the horrors of World War I. [correct]

Use the correct tense when composing a statement made in the past that is true in the present.

> Christopher Columbus sincerely *believed* that the earth *is* round. [Columbus believed this in the past, but it is certainly true today.]

The present tense is acceptable in such situations.

EXERCISE

Correct the following sentences for errors in verb tense. Use C to designate a correct sentence.

1. We have completed the first leg of the relay which was the toughest by far.
2. Abraham Lincoln demonstrated that he felt that slavery is evil.
3. We have completed the first leg of the relay, and we will be running the next soon.
4. Sharon administered first aid just before the lifeguards arrived.
5. After she had mastered French, Phoebe has little difficulty with Spanish.

41
THESIS SENTENCES   ts

The thesis sentence is a sentence that states the central idea of an essay. It is usually clearly expressed in the opening paragraph. The thesis sentence should be specific and concise because it guides the writer and prepares the reader for the content of the essay. A

thesis sentence should not be confused with a topic, which merely announces the subject of the essay.
A thesis statement should do the following:
1. It should narrow your topic to a level that can be adequately developed within your word limit.
2. It should make an assertion about your topic. In so doing, the assertion should reveal your attitude about your topic.
3. It should usually indicate to the reader how you plan to organize the main ideas within the essay.

Notice the differences between topics and thesis sentences in the two examples that follow:

Topic

The Myth of the Phoenix in Eudora Welty's "A Worn Path"

Thesis

The myth of the Phoenix is suggested in Eudora Welty's "A Worn Path" by the theme, the central character, and the bird imagery.

This thesis sentence suggests to the reader that the writer plans to discuss Welty's use of the Phoenix myth in "A Worn Path" with an examination of

1. the theme,
2. the central character,
3. the bird imagery.

Topic

The Prevention of Adolescent Suicide

Thesis

To prevent suicide in adolescents, the public needs to be educated, and potential victims need to be identified and supported.

This writer feels strongly that adolescent suicide is a real problem that can be prevented. He will discuss public education and support of potential victims.

You should also review Introductory and Concluding Paragraphs, p. 137 and the discussion of the thesis sentence in Part 1, pp. 2–3.

EXERCISE

Comment on the effectiveness of the following thesis sentences.

1. Despite all the blatherskite about the new morality, exploitation films — quick-frozen sex and violence — are still the bottom line of the movie biz.
— *Newsweek,* March 15, 1982
2. My generation is special because of what we missed rather than what we got, because in a certain sense we are the first and the last.
— Joyce Maynard
3. Though scoffed at by much of the public as a kind of gladiatorial theater in which showmanship counts far more than genuine athletic skill, professional wrestling enjoys steadily increasing success not only in Houston but in hundreds of tank towns and major cities all over America.
— William C. Martin
4. The Wasps, in fact, are rapidly becoming the one minority that every other ethnic group — blacks, Italians, chicanos, Jews, Poles and all the rest — feels absolutely free to dump on.
— Robert Clairborne

Convert the following topics into thesis sentences:

1. the baseball fan
2. successful parenting
3. fashions
4. marriage
5. high school and college
6. good teaching
7. pornography
8. smoking in public places
9. buying a stereo set
10. guidance counselors

42
USING TRANSITIONS tr

Good writing is coherent when sentences and paragraphs are logically connected. A writer must use transitions to show the relationships between one idea and the next as he moves from sentence to sentence and from paragraph to paragraph. (A more in-depth discussion of the use of transitions to achieve coherence is provided in Paragraph Coherence, p. 131.)

Writers should be aware of the four devices described below that can be used to assure coherence.

Transitional words and phrases

The following is a partial list of some frequently used transitional words and phrases.

after all	meanwhile
also	moreover
and	nevertheless
but	next
consequently	on the other hand
for example	so
however	still
in addition	then
in brief	therefore

Pronoun reference

Clear reference of pronouns to refer to a noun in a previous sentence or paragraph is a means of achieving coherence. (See Paragraph Coherence, p. 131.)

Repetition of key terms

Key terms may be repeated throughout the paragraph to join sentences or to join one paragraph to the next.

Parallelism

The principle of parallelism is that like ideas are expressed in like constructions. Although it is not used as often as the other three devices, parallelism can be used to assure coherence.

For further discussion of transition see the following:
Faulty Parallelism, (**paral//**), p. 97
Paragraph Coherence, (¶ **coh**), p. 131

EXERCISE

All four of the transitional devices discussed above are used in the following paragraph. Try to find examples of each.

> And yet Eastwood's persona is hardly the usual redneck salivating at the prospect of a kill, or even an updated Mike Hammer. Nor would Eastwood be able to command so wide an audience if it were. Whatever the plebian allure, Eastwood has a patrician grace, every inch of a "star," in the old sense, one of the few, I think, to have emerged in America in the last twenty years. The taut, lean, powerfully built body, the sensitively chiseled, unsmiling face, a voice surprisingly soft, almost ghostly in its monosyllabic intonations (though grown thicker and moodier with advancing age), the shock of tawny hair and lithe walk (the most distinctive of any actor's since Fonda), the famous "squint" and glacial eyes which nevertheless can seem terribly vulnerable — these unusual physical endowments couple with Dirty Harry's meager psychological background to produce a certain inarticulate melancholy.
>
> — Robert Mazzocco

43
GLOSSARY OF USAGE | usg

The glossary below provides a selection of words that often confuse college students. Suggestions for correct usage are for standard written English — the level of English found in the writing of educated men and women. In your college and business writing, do not use words that are marked slang or nonstandard in a dictionary.

Many of the glossary words are pairs that writers confuse such as *lie* and *lay, affect* and *effect.* Look over the following entries, then refer to this glossary and a good collegiate dictionary whenever you are in doubt about a particular word. The following are among the desk dictionaries that are particularly useful at the college level:

> *The American Heritage Dictionary of the English Language*
> *Funk and Wagnall's Standard College Dictionary*
> *The Random House Dictionary of the English Language*
> *Webster's New World Dictionary* (3rd ed.)
> *Webster's Ninth New Collegiate Dictionary*

(For a discussion of levels of usage including colloquial, formal, nonstandard, and slang, see Diction, p. 70.)

accept, except. *Accept* is always a verb meaning "to receive." *Except* is a preposition meaning "to exclude."

> I *accept* your donation.
> Everyone was there *except* George.

Occasionally *except* may mean "to leave out."

> The bank *excepted* the interest when she made an early payment.

affect, effect. *Affect* is a verb meaning "to influence." *Effect* is a noun that shows the result of some influence.

> Smoking *affects* the heart and lungs.
> The *effects* of smoking are clear.

Occasionally *effect* is used as a verb meaning "to bring about or achieve."

> Apathetic voters feel that they cannot *effect* a change in government policy.

allusion, illusion. An *allusion* is an indirect reference to something. An *illusion* is a deception or a fantasy.

> He made an *allusion* to Sarah's weak academic background.
> Sarah's confidence created the *illusion* that she had been a good student.

all ready, already. *All ready* means "fully prepared to do something." *Already* is an adverb meaning "before this time."

> The players were *all ready* to board the bus.
> Your package has *already* been shipped, sir.

all right, alright. *All right* is always two words. *Alright* is nonstandard for *all right*.

among, between. *Among* is used with more than two persons or things. *Between* should be used only when two persons or things are involved.

> There was discord *among* the members of the surveying club.
> Jason couldn't decide *between* shrimp and clams.

It is becoming generally acceptable to use *between* when *among* sounds awkward.

as, like. See **like, as.**

bad, badly. Use *bad* as an adjective, *badly* as an adverb.

> I feel *bad* today. [Here *bad* refers to health.]
> Mr. Jones behaved *badly* when he lost the tennis match.

beside, besides. *Beside* means "at the side of"; *besides* means "in addition to."

> The boy lies *beside* the bed.
> *Besides* being attractive, Becky is a good student.

better, best. Use *better* when comparing two persons or things; *best* with more than two.

> Matt is a *better* tennis player than Bill.
> Gladys is the *best* tennis player in the city.

can, may. In formal usage, *can* expresses ability and *may* expresses permission.

43 / Glossary of Usage

John *can* run five miles in thirty minutes.
May I watch his next race?

cite, site. *Cite* is a verb meaning "to mention or point to." *Site* is a noun meaning "a particular place."

I plan to *cite* three examples of ineffective advertising.
The architect wants to build on the *site* in the center of town.

complement, compliment. *Complement* is a noun or a verb meaning "to complete." *Compliment* means "to praise or flatter."

Transitive verbs cannot stand alone. They need *complements* to complete their meaning.
I *compliment* you on your fine family.

continual, continuous. *Continual* means "repeatedly." *Continuous* means without interruption.

Watching a movie on television is frustrating because of the *continual* interruptions of commercials and the telephone.
The new dam will provide the area with a *continuous* flow of water.

differ from, differ with. To *differ from* means "to be different." To *differ with* means "to disagree."

The houses *differ from* each other in their entries and back porches.
The two candidates *differ with* each other on the issue of gun control.

disinterested, uninterested. *Disinterested* means "unbiased," "objective." *Uninterested* means "lacking interest."

Three *disinterested* spectators volunteered to umpire the game.

Judy said that she failed because she was *uninterested* in the course.

due to the fact that. This is a wordy construction; use *because*.

farther, further. *Farther* usually refers to additional distance. *Further* refers to additional time or amount.

It is much *farther* to drive to Indiana than I expected.
It is late and we cannot discuss the issue *further*.

effect. See **affect, effect.**

except. See **accept, except.**

explicit, implicit. *Explicit* means "not held back." *Implicit* means "left unstated."

Many R-rated movies contain *explicit* sex and violence.
Mary thought that she had an *implicit* understanding with her daughter that she would not take the family car without permission.

good, well. *Good* is an adjective; *well* is generally an adverb except when it refers to health.

The center is a *good* rebounder. [adjective]
The team plays *well* when all of the players feel *well*. [The first *well* is an adverb; the second *well* is an adjective.]
You look *well*. [adverb meaning healthy]
You look *good*. [adjective meaning attractive]

hanged, hung. *Hanged* is used only when it refers to an execution. *Hung* is used in all other situations.

The cattle rustler was sentenced to be *hanged* from the gallows.
The ornaments were *hung* from the tree.

illusion. See **allusion, illusion.**

imply, infer. *Imply* means "to suggest"; *infer* means "to conclude." Speakers *imply* and listeners *infer*.

The minister *implied* that he would finish his sermon in a few minutes.

The audience *inferred* that the minister's conclusion would follow.

irregardless. *Irregardless* is nonstandard among educated speakers and writers. Use *regardless*.

lie, lay. *Lie* is an intransitive verb that means "to rest or recline"; *lay* is a transitive verb that means "to set or place."

INFINITIVE	PAST TENSE	PAST PARTICIPLE	PRESENT PARTICIPLE
to lie	lay	lain	lying
to lay	laid	laid	laying

Gramps thought that he would *lie* down for a nap.

I thought that he *laid* the package on the kitchen counter, but instead he said it was lying on the top shelf.

like, as. Use *like* as a preposition when making comparisons. Use *as* as a conjunction to introduce a dependent clause.

Like a clutch player, Julius Erving always looks for the shot when the game is close.

As she usually does, my French teacher reviewed the vocabulary before the test.

principle, principal. *Principle* is always a noun meaning "rule of truth." As a noun, *principal* means "ruling authority" or "capital investment." As an adjective, *principal* means "main."

As a matter of *principle,* Rod would not pay his friend a compliment.

The *principal* idea was to persuade the school board that the dress code was unfair.

The *principal* of our school is Mr. Rogers.

quotation, quote. *Quotation* is always a noun; *quote* is always a verb. The use of *quote* as a noun is colloquial.

"I used three direct *quotes* in my research paper." [colloquial. It should be "three direct *quotations*."]

Stan *quotes* Churchill three times in his paper.

raise, rise. *Raise* is a transitive verb and it must have a direct object. You *raise* something. *Rise* is intransitive and does not need a direct object.

My friend *raises* Irish setters.

I *rise* at 5:00 A.M.

Infinitive	Past Tense	Past Participle	Present Participle
to raise	raised	raised	raising
to rise	rose	risen	rising

sensual, sensuous. *Sensual* is an adjective that has to do with sexuality. *Sensuous* refers to the sense impressions in general.

The actor gave a *sensual* performance in the love scene.

The poet's *sensuous* imagery calls upon our senses of sight, taste, and smell.

set, sit. *Set* is a transitive verb meaning "to place." *Sit* is an intransitive verb meaning "to recline in a chair."

Larry will *set* the pitcher of beer on the table before he *sits* down.

their, there, they're. *Their* is a possessive adjective or pronoun. *There* refers to place, or is an expletive. *They're* is a contraction for "they are."

Their dog is in the house.

She will stay *there*.
There is nothing we can do about it.
T̲hey're leaving in an hour or so.

then, than. *Then* is generally an adverb related to time and *than* is a conjunction that suggests comparisons.

The jury knew *then* that the defendant was more violent *than* it had suspected.

to, too, two. *To* is a preposition and an infinitive marker, *too* is an adverb, and *two* is a number.

I would like *to* buy *two* books *to* give *to* my friend if they don't cost *too* much.

uninterested. See **disinterested, uninterested.**

44
SENTENCE VARIETY | var

A sequence of sentences following the same pattern is monotonous. To make your writing more interesting you should vary your sentences by mixing short sentences with longer ones. Often it is useful to vary the word order. Before we consider how to achieve variety in sentence structure, let's first look at what to avoid.

The paragraph below is monotonous because the sentence patterns and length are much the same.

Harold's opponents hinted that the haste of his coronation   1
was indecent. It looked as if he had been afraid that someone   2
else would snatch the crown from him. But there was a good   3
traditional reason for doing it then and there. Coronations   4
were held at the great feasts of the church. The funeral was   5
on Epiphany. The coronation was done the same afternoon   6
because, if not, the bishop would have wanted to wait until
Easter. This would leave the kingdom without a head for   7
three months.

Although this paragraph is perfectly clear and is full of details, it is monotonous because six of the seven sentences are simple sentences. Compare the choppy paragraph above with the actual paragraph below.

> Long afterwards, his opponents hinted that the haste of it was indecent, as if he had been afraid someone else would snatch the crown from him. But there was a good traditional reason for doing it then and there. Coronations were held at the great feasts of the church, and the funeral was on Epiphany; if it had not been done that same afternoon, the bishop would have wanted to wait until Easter, leaving the kingdom without a head for what might be a difficult three months.
>
> — David Howarth

You will notice that the style in the actual paragraph is smoother and more sophisticated. The difference is that the second paragraph employs sentence variety. It contains three sentences (rather than seven), and it uses subordination and coordination effectively. The only simple sentence in the paragraph is the second, and it describes a transitional point that Howarth wishes to emphasize.

But there was a good traditional reason for doing it then and there.

You should review sections on coordination, pp. 65–67, and subordination, pp. 153–156.

To achieve sentence variety, writers should try to do the following.

Vary sentence structure and length. Use simple sentences, but use them to emphasize significant points. Be aware that compound, complex, and compound-complex sentences join equal or independent clauses and subordinate dependent clauses.

Vary sentence beginnings. Note that in the first example above, the monotonous effect is the result of two problems: (1) too many simple sentences, and (2) too much repetition of the same pattern. Six of the seven simple sentences begin with the subject that is followed by the verb that is followed by the object. Writers can effectively avoid the overuse of the subject-verb-object pattern by shifting modifiers to the beginning of the sentence. Observe how the sentence beginnings shift in the following sentences.

Struggling during the examination, the students were unaware of the fire in the building across the street.

Unaware of the fire in the building across the street, the students struggled during the examination.

There were students struggling during the examination who were unaware of the fire in the building across the street.

For further discussion of related issues see the following sections:

Part 2, Sentence Types, pp. 38–39
Faulty Coordination, (**coord**), p. 65
Faulty Subordination, (**sub**), p. 153

EXERCISE

Vary the sentence structure by following the directions in the parentheses after the sentences below.

1. The mountain climbers sheltered themselves from the blizzard in a cave that was near the summit. (vary beginning)
2. World oil prices have been stable for months. Last week they began to fall. Mexico and Venezuela cut their prices. The move left the oil market in disarray. (vary sentence structure)
3. Last semester I had a good schedule. My first class was at 9:00. I had a break for two hours for lunch. My last class was over before 4:00. (vary sentence structure)
4. David realized that the river was dangerous; nevertheless, he decided not to cancel the canoe trip that he had been planning since last winter. (vary beginning)

Comment on the effectiveness of the sentence variety in the following paragraph.

We also felt that the writing of history has suffered in recent years because some historians have been overly eager to convert their discipline into an unadulterated social science. Undeniably, history would lose much of its claim to contemporary relevance without the methods and theories it has borrowed from anthropology, psychology, political science, economics, sociology, and other fields. Yet history is rooted in the narrative tradition. As much as it seeks to generalize from past events, as do the sciences, it also remains dedicated to capturing the uniqueness of a situation. When historians neglect the literary aspect of their discipline — when they forget that good history begins with a good story — they risk losing the wider audience that all great historians have addressed. They end up sadly, talking to themselves.

— Janes West Davidson
Mark Hamilton Lytle

45
WORDY — UNNECESSARY REPETITION w/rep

Writers tend to use more words than needed to say what has to be said. Good writing should be concise and precise. You should decide what you mean and say it directly. Early drafts are almost always more wordy than revisions, and an important part of the revision process is to substitute exact words and phrases for empty words and needless repetition. Many writers find that it is helpful to set a goal by eliminating, say, twenty-five or thirty percent of the words in an early draft. You will soon discover that a wordy sentence such as:

John walked angrily out of his chemistry lab.

can be improved with the use of a strong verb:

John stormed out of his chemistry lab.

The following faults are among the trouble spots that contribute to wordiness.

Avoid stock phrases.

STOCK PHRASE	SUBSTITUTE
come to a conclusion	conclude
due to the fact that	because
in many instances	often
in the near future	soon
absolutely essential	essential
in this day and age	today

45 / Wordy—Unnecessary Repetition   w/rep

Change clauses to phrases, phrases to single words.

WORDY

The man *who owns the flower shop* is seven feet tall.

BETTER

The owner *of the flower shop* is seven feet tall.

BEST

The *florist* is seven feet tall.

Avoid the passive voice. Passive voice is always more wordy than active voice.

The students *were frustrated by* the test.

The test *frustrated* the students.

For further information on the passive voice, see Ineffective Use of Passive Voice, p. 140.

Avoid unnecessary repetition. Words and phrases should not be repeated unnecessarily because then they draw needless attention to themselves as illustrated in the examples below.

FAULTY

Becky considered the opportunity of travelling to Scotland a valuable opportunity.

CORRECT

Becky considered travelling to Scotland a valuable opportunity.

FAULTY

We planned to meet just after dark in the evening.

CORRECT

We planned to meet just after dark.

FAULTY

The monument on the town square adds much beauty to the town square.

CORRECT

The monument adds much beauty to the town square.

w/rep | 174 | An Alphabetical List of Frequent Writing Problems

The most common kind of needless repetition is the redundant phrase (such as *surrounding environment* and *large in size*, which say the same thing twice.) Here are some more examples of redundant phrases.

lovely in appearance
real and true
biography of his life
cooperate together
warm and friendly
round in shape

Repetition in writing can be effective, however, when it is used for emphasis, parallel structure, and paragraph coherence. (See Faulty Parallelism, p. 97 and Paragraph Unity, p. 127.)

John was a good citizen and loyal father. He was proud of his family, proud of his community, and proud of his country. [The repetition of *proud* emphasizes the parallel structure of the three phrases.]

For further discussion of related topics see the following sections:

Faulty Parallelism, (**paral //**), p. 97
Paragraph Coherence, (**coh**), p. 131

EXERCISE

Revise the sentences below to avoid unnecessary repetition. Correct them with concise and direct language.

1. Due to the fact that his fairy tales are so widely read, Hans Christian Andersen is Denmark's most famous author.
2. Andersen, who was the son of a poor shoemaker, wrote with wisdom and simplicity. In all probability he wrote to adults as well as children because his stories often have complex meanings that are intended for adult readers.
3. Old age and childhood are two stages in life that are very similar in many ways. The life of a child and the life of an elderly person have much in common.

4. An elderly person acts like a child in many ways. One very common trait they both have is a world of fantasy.
5. In many instances elderly people and children both have very sensitive emotions.
6. Debbie and Becky must learn to cooperate together if they are to finish the job by sunset.
7. The pilot steered abruptly; his steering made my brother ill.
8. He feels that after the heat of the immediate conflict that both parties will resolve the strike threat.
9. In Maria's mind she thinks that Tom should apologize.
10. The faculty council felt that students do not take advantage of the advantages given to them.

4
Writing the Research Paper

The methods for writing a research paper described in this Part follow guidelines established in 1984 by the Modern Language Association. The 1984 guidelines differ markedly from previous *MLA Handbook* recommendations, most noticeably in the style for documentation. In general, the revised guidelines stress brevity, and writers should find that using these guidelines simplifies the composition of the research paper. Although the new methods continue to provide for the necessary accuracy, they also make possible a more efficient presentation. As always, however, students should pay close attention to the details of form in documentation and bibliographical entries, for the new methods are simpler but no less demanding in their attention to detail.

DEFINING THE RESEARCH PAPER

A research paper is a formal essay in which the author seeks to prove a thesis partly by providing evidence gathered from outside sources. This definition is worth examining closely.

Because it is a *formal essay*, the research paper must follow all the rules governing essays (essay form, thesis and topic sentences, standard conventions of grammar and syntax, etc.). The research paper is not a business or technical report, and it is not an informal essay, which conveys a tone better suited to other purposes.

Since the author seeks to prove a thesis only *partly* by providing evidence gathered from outside sources, a research paper is not a mere collection of quotations and facts, a "cut-and-paste" project. The author must have an original thesis, and all evidence must serve the purpose of proving that thesis. Evidence is a tool; it is not an end in itself.

Evidence is gathered from *outside sources* which include books, magazines, newspapers, pamphlets, and other printed material. Evidence can also come from interviews, films, records, tapes, and personal documents. All evidence must be verifiable, and for this reason, the research paper includes documentation of all sources of evidence.

In judging the success or failure of a research paper, the writer should consider one central question: How useful is the paper? This question affects both the author and reader.

From the author's standpoint, the research paper provides a clear system for exploring a topic. Because all research papers are produced through the systematic process described in this Part, the author's job is simplified. What to do first and what to do second and so on, what to include or not to include, how to present the finished paper — all these problems and many others can be avoided by following the system. The research paper also enhances the author's claim to authority on the chosen topic. The paper says, in effect, "I've studied my topic thoroughly. I know what I'm talking about."

From the reader's standpoint, the research paper should be useful because it provides information in a standard form. All the rules for a research paper exist so that a standard form is possible. If form is correct, then the reader can use the paper itself as evidence for some other purpose, or the reader can easily consult listed sources for more information on certain points.

No matter what the topic is, students composing research papers should remember that they are working with a system, and that system exists to help everyone.

CHOOSING A TOPIC

Sometimes an instructor will provide a specific topic for a research paper. More often, however, you are given a general subject, and the task of limiting it is left to you. While exploring the subject, ask three questions each time you consider a possible topic.

1. Can I do justice to the topic in the amount of space and time I have available? Some topics are too complicated to discuss in papers of ten or twenty pages — or even longer. "World War II," for example, is a topic simply too broad for anything but book-length treatment, and researching such a topic would take years. A research paper should make a worthwhile contribution to your reader's understanding. A sketchy presentation has little value.
2. Can I find enough research material on the topic? If the topic is too narrow, you are likely to find only a few sources of material, if any. "Building model airplanes" is such a topic. Don't be misled into thinking that a topic is suitable simply because you have seen one or two articles on the subject. In fact, all research material on such a limited topic is likely to present the same information. Also, do not choose a topic so new that little has been published on it.
3. Can I say anything new on the topic? If you cannot provide a fresh insight, your audience is likely to be uninterested from the start. Although "The dangers of drunken driving" is a topic that points to an important issue, your own contribution to the reader's knowledge will probably be minimal.

Remember that in the early stages of composing a research paper, you can adjust the topic you've chosen. If you discover a fault in the topic, you are much better off changing direction rather than pursuing an unreachable goal.

EXERCISE

Decide which of the following possible topics would be suitable for a research paper of seven to twelve pages. Be prepared to discuss why each topic is or is not appropriate.

1. Job opportunities for speech therapists
2. Football has an interesting history
3. Developments in cancer research
4. Television news
5. The dangers of smoking
6. Rock and roll music developed from rhythm and blues
7. Types of sails for board sailing

8. Winston Churchill
9. Alternative energy
10. The Negro Spiritual as protest literature

RESEARCHING THE TOPIC

When you begin research, the process of organizing information becomes crucial. You must know what information to record, how to record it, and how to keep track of what you have already recorded. Note cards offer a useful tool in this process because they can be arranged and rearranged without trouble. Also, adding to a stack of cards is much easier than trying to fit extra information on to pages of notes, which can soon become confusing and difficult to read. As you check sources, remember that the cards you are preparing will be indispensable when you begin writing the paper itself.

Prepare a working bibliography

The working bibliography is a collection of sources that might offer useful information on your topic. For each possible source, prepare a card, using the citation forms that appear on pp. 198–205 of this chapter. Two sample cards appear below, one for a book and the other for an article. The card for the book also includes the library call number.

FOR A BOOK

library call # missing

Veatch, Robert M. *Death, Dying, and the Biological Revolution.* New Haven: Yale UP, 1976.

FOR AN ARTICLE

> Hotchkiss, Sandy. "Peaceful
> Dying, a Human Approach
> to the Terminally Ill."
> *Human Behavior* Apr. 1978: 32.

In the library, research sources are most commonly identified in three places:

Card catalogue. This catalogue contains author, title, and subject cards listing the library's circulating collection. Remember, however, that libraries vary in what materials they possess. One library might own many books on a certain subject while another library might own few or none. As a result, the card catalogue in any one library is not always a good indicator of how much material might be available on a given subject. Encyclopedia articles usually name other sources of information, and often books you locate on your subject will include their own bibliographies of related sources. There are, in addition, guides that list titles of books. Two of the better known are the yearly *Books in Print* directories and *The Library of Congress Catalog of Books: Subjects* (1950–present).

Some libraries today are augmenting or phasing out their card catalogues by using computers to store information about their holdings. Be just as careful in using the computer as you would be in using the card catalogue.

Periodical indexes. These indexes list articles that have appeared in periodicals and magazines. There are many such indexes. The one best known is the *Readers' Guide to Periodical Literature,* but special indexes can often be more valuable because of their limited scope. If, for example, your topic concerns agriculture, the *Biological and Agricultural Index* will be far more useful than an index designed to cover as many subjects as possible. Always consult with the reference librarian to see if a specialized index exists that might give you access to material you otherwise would never know about.

Pamphlet and document files. Many libraries have files in which pamphlets and documents are organized by subject. In addition to containing valuable sources, these files can suggest other possible sources of information. If your subject is nuclear power, you might discover a pamphlet published by an organization devoted to studying the issue of nuclear power. If time permits, you could even contact such an organization for more material.

Libraries also contain dictionaries, encyclopedias, atlases, and other useful sources. Remember too that throughout the entire process of locating research sources, the reference librarian can be extremely helpful. If you have questions about where to look, this librarian can quickly direct you and save much time and trouble.

Judge the sources

As you research sources, judge them by asking how authoritative they are. The answer to this question is important because your own authority on the topic is enhanced if your sources are generally acknowledged as reliable, but your authority can be challenged if you cite sources that themselves are open to question. A first step in judging material is to distinguish primary sources from secondary sources.

Primary sources. People and organizations who are closest to your topic are known as primary sources. If the topic involves public education, you may find that statistical reports of test scores, personal interviews, and student handbooks are useful; and as primary sources, they will carry weight because they have not been interpreted by someone else. Using them in the research paper lets you move close to the topic's point of origin. If your topic concerns Robert Frost, Frost's poems, Frost's published and unpublished letters, and Frost's manuscripts all would qualify as primary sources.

Secondary sources. These sources are a step or more removed from the topic's point of origin. They consist of someone else's interpretation of sources and comments on those sources. Books about public education written by teachers and administrators would most likely qualify as secondary sources on the topic. Articles on Frost's poetry and biographies of his life are also examples of secondary sources of information. No matter what the topic is, the closer the writer moves to the topic's point of origin, the more authority the research paper will have. In addition, factual errors become more likely as information passes from place to place, so it is safer to stay close to the topic's origin.

Aside from distinguishing primary and secondary sources, be sure the sources are not dated. If the topic is medical technology, a ten-year-old book describing operating room equipment might already be unreliable. You should also recognize the possibility that a source might be biased. Interviews with crime victims could be useful in discussion of the criminal justice system, but keep in mind that the people interviewed have a very personal involvement with the topic. Bias itself is not always a problem, but not recognizing possible bias is always detrimental to your presentation.

Prepare a tentative thesis and outline

You should formulate your thesis during the research process. As you read, try as soon as possible to find the controlling idea that you believe can serve as the thesis for the paper, and put this idea in writing. If you trust it to memory, you can forget it. Furthermore, writing down a tentative thesis sentence will help you see what goal you have in mind, and will focus your reading of sources. Also, writing the tentative thesis shows that you *do* know what central idea you intend to prove. If you find it impossible to write such a sentence, the message should be clear: you need to do more reading and thinking about the topic.

The final thesis should be the product of two activities: researching sources and thinking about what the sources reveal. So once you have a tentative thesis sentence on paper, be prepared to rewrite it later. As you continue reading and begin taking notes, new ideas might appear, or certain ideas might become more (or less) important. In general, you will have arrived at a good thesis when you have written a brief statement of what you believe is true about your topic and which you are sure can be supported by outside sources.

Composing a thesis sentence is the last step in a process of limiting, a process that began with a general subject. That subject is limited to a topic. The topic is then limited further — to a thesis sentence. For more discussion of the thesis sentence, see pp. 158–160.

Establishing a thesis makes forming an outline easier. Look for ideas that can be grouped. Connections will begin to appear, and a preliminary outline can take shape and help guide you in the research process. The outline you compose during research can be adjusted to fit the tentative thesis, and the thesis itself can change to accommodate the plan that evolves for structuring the paper. The main point to remember is that while research is in progress, both the thesis and the outline are tentative and, therefore, flexible.

In the previous section on preparing a working bibliography, two sample note cards appear for a research project whose general subject was "death and dying." As the student began research, he quickly noticed that many sources referred to a changing attitude toward death and dying, and he realized that this changing attitude might provide a suitable topic for his research paper. He continued reading sources and gradually decided that defining the new attitude would be worthwhile. He also saw that in order to be convincing, he needed to identify the attitude, explain why it had developed, and provide illustrations of the new attitude in action. All these ideas led to a tentative thesis: "Society has never before made an effort to understand the process of dying, but because we are now making the effort, we fear death less, and we can help those who are dying." The tentative outline read as follows:

    I. Our new attitude has centered on overcoming resistance to discussing death and dying.
   II. This change has been prompted by medical advances.
  III. The new attitude is obvious in its many manifestations.

With a tentative thesis and outline, the student had a valuable tool for continuing his research. He knew what point he wanted to prove and how to go about offering proof. Further research enabled the student to refine the thesis and make the outline more specific.

Researching the Topic 185

Take notes on the sources

Systematically gathering information becomes possible once a tentative thesis and outline are established, and note cards again become useful. As you take notes, identify sources by using the methods of documentation that appear on pp. 190–197 of this Part. Using proper documentation forms at this stage will save time when you write the paper itself because you won't need to relocate information — everything you need will appear on the cards. The note card will list the source material and its precise location in the source, and the bibliography card (see pp. 180–181) will contain all information needed for the list of works cited of the finished paper. So as you record your notes on cards, each source will have one bibliography card and as many note cards as you feel are necessary.

Three types of notes are most common: direct quotations, paraphrasings, and summaries. Each serves its own purpose, and each requires careful attention to the research material and to your own reading and understanding of that material.

Direct quotation. A direct quotation is an exact restatement. When taking information from sources, be sure to place quotation marks around anything you copy word for word so as to identify it as an exact restatement. For a further discussion on the use of quotation marks, see Uses of Quotation Marks, p. 117.

A note card with a direct quotation might look like this:

(Ogg 2)

"American culture with its stress on winning, shapes these physicians [who treat the dying], as it does the rest of us. Death is an enemy to be held at bay as long as possible — even denied. Professionally committed to saving lives and equipped as they now are with elaborate medical technology, doctors — and many nurses too — have regarded death as the ultimate failure."

In this quotation, using brackets to identify the physicians was necessary to clarify the source's meaning. Anytime there is a need to insert clarifying information, enclose the information in brackets, *not* parentheses. For a further discussion of use of brackets, see Uses of Brackets, p. 116.

Paraphrasing. A paraphrasing is a restatement in the researcher's own words of another person's presentation. A note card carrying a paraphrasing might look like the following example where the student has paraphrased the information directly quoted on the previous card:

> (Ogg 2)
>
> American culture stresses winning. This stress affects doctors who treat the dying as well as the rest of us. Death is an enemy, and doctors (and many nurses) have regarded death as the ultimate failure.

When you write your research paper, use the paraphrase when you see no need to quote directly. The paraphrase also provides variety and can help minimize the stylistic error of sounding as though you have simply assembled a collection of other people's words and ideas.

Summary. A summary condenses a long passage and can be an efficient way to present information that could slow down your presentation. A summary appears on p. 6 of the sample research paper at the end of this Part (p. 225), and the original passage appears on the facing page.

One further point about the technique of note-taking is worth mentioning here: Never try to fit all notes from one source on one card. Instead, put only one idea on each card because this will simplify the process of ordering the note cards when you write the paper, especially if you use different material from one source in different parts of the paper.

Work carefully to avoid plagiarism

Plagiarism is the use of information or ideas that have not been clearly identified as originating with someone else. Plagiarism can take many forms, most of which can be grouped under the two headings described below.

An unacknowledged quotation. If you include words, sentences, or data in your paper that are not common knowledge but which you have discovered in an outside source, you must acknowledge the source with correct documentation. Failing to do so constitutes plagiarism.

A "borrowed" idea. An unacknowledged quotation is obvious theft. Sometimes, however, a writer is tempted to use someone else's imagination without giving credit. This too is plagiarism. For example, if your topic is reform of laws regulating American factory safety, you might read an article in which the author organizes his material by presenting three views of factory safety: those of the factory owner, the factory worker, and the general public. The idea for this structure has originated with the author of the article. It thus must be treated as *his* idea. Should *you* then write your own paper and employ this same structure, you must acknowledge your debt. Even if your discussion of each of the three points presents your own original work, the overall plan you are following is not your own, and you must state this fact. Acknowledgement in this case should be stated in the text of the paper itself. Do not use a note in such cases because it unfairly downplays the importance of the idea you have borrowed and used for your own purposes.

The "borrowed" idea can result from another problem. As work on a research project progresses, it is easy to become confused about where ideas have originated. For example, if your topic focuses on a literary work, you will no doubt read a great deal of published criticism of the work, and this reading will probably enhance your understanding. Such understanding is desirable, but when you write your own paper, the many ideas — ideas originating with other people — can become a swirl of memories in which critics, published criticism, and your own ideas are indistinguishable. Avoiding this intractable problem is possible if you use note cards not only for quotations, paraphrasings, and summaries, but also for important ideas that might be included in your paper. A note such as *Plath — confusing motive and art, real and ideal, p. 83* can be enough to remind you where to relocate a useful idea, and can also remind you of just who originated the idea.

Two other facts about plagiarism deserve mention. First, you might not intend to plagiarize. However, plagiarism lies not in what you *intend* but in what you actually *do*. Even if plagiarism results from an honest mistake on your part, you will still be held accountable. As with all writing, once the words are on paper and the paper is in the hands of another person, what you intended to do is immaterial. The *paper* speaks to your audience, not you, and the audience is able to judge only what it reads.

Second, plagiarism serves no useful purpose, particularly in a research paper where part of your own authority on a topic results from demonstrating your study of research material. Acknowledging all sources is to your advantage — and is an easy process if reading and note-taking are done carefully.

COMPOSING A FORMAL OUTLINE

Your instructor may require a formal outline with your research paper. Regardless of requirements, however, composing an outline before writing the first draft is clearly to your advantage, for an outline will allow you to sort and arrange the many ideas that must be logically presented in the final paper. Writing a research paper is a far more elaborate undertaking than writing a short, informal essay or a short story. You must keep ideas distinct from each other, maintain coherence among ideas, and order the ideas logically. These, of course, are the same tasks anyone faces when writing, but the larger scale of a research paper makes the job more complex. A good outline can make these tasks easier and also save time.

A *topic outline* expresses main and subordinate ideas in phrases. A *sentence outline* expresses main and subordinate ideas

Composing a Formal Outline

in complete sentences and is especially valuable because it allows you to compose, in advance, tentative topic sentences for the various sections of the research paper. Once the outline is complete, the skeleton for the paper is ready so that writing the first draft is a far less difficult process.

No matter which type of outline you compose, you should follow standard form in its presentation:

    I. ....
       A. ....
       B. ....
          1. ....
          2. ....
             a. ....
             b. ....
   II. ....

When an outline is complete, the relationships of main and subordinate ideas should be clear. Each indentation denotes a subheading in which subordinate ideas are grouped under a main idea, and the scope of each main idea (how much it encompasses) is obvious. Each *A* is supported by *1, 2,* etc., and each *1* is supported by *a, b,* etc.

To check the logic of an outline, ask these three questions:

1. Are ideas of equal weight placed in parallel positions? In other words, is *I* equal in importance to *II*? Is the same true of *A* and *B* and *C* and so on? If parallel structure is sound, then emphasis in the paper can be properly distributed. Main ideas can sound like main ideas because they are emphasized and parallel.
2. Have I included all information on one idea in one place? Answering this question will reveal how carefully you have grouped related ideas. Here, an outline serves the invaluable purpose of letting you see, ahead of time, how the parts of the paper will fit together.
3. Have I avoided single subheadings? If you list subheading *A*, you must list at least *B*. If you list *1*, you must list at least *2*. The logic of this requirement becomes apparent if you remember that the outline shows how ideas are divided. Nothing can be divided into one part.

The outline provided for the sample research paper at the end of this Part shows how a careful outline is constructed. This outline makes clear what the paper covers, how the material is arranged, and how main and subordinate ideas relate to each other — the three aspects of a paper which any outline should communicate to the reader.

WRITING THE FIRST DRAFT

Writing the first draft of a research paper requires all the skills necessary to write any essay. Because the research paper is a special kind of essay, however, it makes additional demands. As you write, keep in mind the recommendations given in the following paragraphs.

Make good use of the space available. A research paper will probably be longer than most other essays you write. You can, therefore, easily avoid the stylistic mistake of sounding rushed. Do not waste time, but move smoothly, particularly in the introduction and conclusion. Extensive discussion of a topic needs deliberation and patience, and an abrupt beginning or ending can damage your entire presentation.

Reaffirm the thesis periodically. This keeps the reader on track and is important when you are presenting a lengthy discussion. Avoid mechanically restating the thesis, but find ways to refer to it at appropriate points. Any essay must be unified, and unifying a long essay requires careful attention.

Compose a true essay, not a mere list of quotations and references. A serious error exists if the reader has the impression that you have simply strung together pieces of information.

Incorporate quotations smoothly. Never jam quotations into your discussion. Use the ellipsis cautiously, if necessary, to tailor quotations so that all sentences flow naturally. For a discussion of the ellipsis, see Uses of the Ellipsis Mark, p. 124.

Be sure to document all material that needs documentation. You must provide documentation for all ideas and information you take from outside sources. In addition, the reader must be able to tell exactly where your words end and the borrowed words begin. Incorporate source material carefully to avoid uncertainty.

Use proper methods of documentation. The methods of documentation now recommended by the *MLA Handbook* differ greatly from the older, more complex methods they replace. The new, simpler methods call for short, precise identification of sources in the text of the paper itself, *not* in endnotes or footnotes. The following examples illustrate the new documentation style, and a detailed explanation follows them.

Suppose you are writing a research paper on French history, and you wish to quote from page 153 of the book *Voltaire: A Biography* by Haydn Mason. Your paper might state the following:

```
Voltaire's popularity during his own lifetime was

immense, but "It is with the early period of the

Revolution that Voltaire's influence can be most

closely associated. . . ." (Mason 153).
```

Note that the author's last name and the page reference are given in parentheses rather than by using a number in superscript and a footnote or endnote.

Another method for incorporating the source material is to include the author's name in your text:

```
Voltaire's popularity during his own lifetime was

immense, but as Haydn Mason states, "It is with the

early period of the Revolution that Voltaire's in-

fluence can be most closely associated. . . ." (153).
```

Note that the author's name is not repeated in the parenthetical documentation.

With either method, a person reading such a statement in your paper is informed of the quotation's author and precise location in the source. The reader can consult the Works Cited page where entries are listed alphabetically, and he can easily find complete identifying information for the source. The Works Cited entry that follows is for the work cited in the above examples:

Mason, Haydn. <u>Voltaire: A Biography</u>. Baltimore:
Johns Hopkins UP, 1981.

All documentation should now be written this way. The following guidelines provide a more detailed explanation of the revised style.

The name of the source must be given either in the text of your paper or in the parenthetical documentation. The reader must be able to locate the source in the list of works cited, quickly and without confusion.

When documenting a source written by two or three authors where the names of the authors are not given in your text, include the last names of the authors in the parentheses:

> Among the many facts about language, three stand
> out: language is human, language is thought and
> activity, and the medium of language is sound
> (Bolinger and Sears 2-3).

Note that a comma is not used between the authors' names and the page reference and that the abbreviation "pp" is omitted. A reader seeing such a statement would know that the borrowed material appears on pages 2 and 3 of the source, and the list of works cited entry for the source would provide full information:

> Bolinger, Dwight, and Donald A. Sears. <u>Aspects of
> Language</u>. 3rd ed. New York: Harcourt, 1981.

When listing a work by more than three authors, the Works Cited entry will name only the first author and then will state "et al." (meaning "and others"). When using parenthetical documentation for such a source, state the last name of the first author, then "et al.," then the page number(s):

> (Aiken et al. 288)

This style for the documentation entry agrees with the style for the Works Cited entry:

> Aiken, Geoffrey, et al. <u>Business Applications for the 1980's</u>. New York: Gables, 1983.

If necessary, document the source title. For example, if you are citing more than one work by the same author, your paper might read:

> Kenneth Clark discusses the painter Giotto and focuses on Giotto's <u>Lamentation of the Dead Christ</u>. The painting, according to Clark, is "one of the supreme compositions in art. . . ." (<u>What Is a Masterpiece?</u> 19), a work "which foreshadows the carefully constructed compositions of the later Giotto, but is still painted with a passion and spontaneity that they seem to lack. . . ." (<u>Civilisation</u> 84).

The reader of such a statement would know the precise location of each quotation in each source and would find detailed information about the sources on the Works Cited page:

> Clark, Kenneth. <u>Civilisation</u>. New York: Harper, 1969.
>
> ---. <u>What Is a Masterpiece?</u> New York: Thames and Hudson, 1979.

Sometimes documenting by title is necessary because no author is given in the source, and the Works Cited page lists the source by title. For example:

Philippine politics were noteworthy throughout 1983, and in March 1984, tens of thousands of Filipinos spent seven days marching from the provinces to a huge rally in Manila ("Foes").

The reader consulting the Works Cited page would find the following entry:

"Foes of Marcos Stage Huge Anti-election Rally."
Boston Globe 8 March 1984: 4.

Since the newspaper article used in this example appears only on one page of the newspaper issue (page 4), including a page number in the documentation is unnecessary. If the entire article appeared on more than one page, however, including a page number in the documentation would be required so that the precise location of the material being cited is identified.

When documenting, use short versions of long titles in the parenthesis. The example given above includes documentation of a source whose title is so long that writing out the entire title would make documentation unwieldy. Thus, the short version "Foes" is preferable. Most long titles can be shortened: *Long Walks in the Afternoon* can become *Long Walks; The Origins of the English Civil War* can be documented as *Origins*. Remember that short versions are acceptable *only in the parenthesis used to document sources*. Everywhere else in the text of your paper — and in the Works Cited list — you must write out titles in full.

When documenting volume and page numbers of a multivolume work, add the volume number to the documentation:

(Evans 2: 133)

This citation denotes page 133 of volume 2 of Evans' work. Omit the words "volume" and "page" (or their abbreviations). If you need to document an entire volume, place a comma after the author's name, skip one space, and use the abbreviation "vol." (note use of lowercase "v") before the page number:

    (Evans, vol. 2)

When documenting more than one source in a single reference, list each source as you usually would, but separate each source with a semicolon:

    (Flynn 318; Fennell 77-79)

    (Skrekas and Athanas 280; McGarry

    et al. 74; <u>Adolescent Years</u> 38-41)

Design your presentation so that documentation can be exact but brief. For example:

    Carl Sagan offers an understandable description of

    the age of the universe in <u>The Dragons of Eden</u>.

    Sagan compresses the fifteen-billion-year lifetime

    of the universe into the span of a single year and

    gives a monthly account of how the universe evolved

    (13-17). On such a calendar, human intelligence

    appears only very late in December (102), and "It

    is only in the last day. . .that substantial intel-

    lectual abilities have evolved on the planet

    Earth" (238).

The documentation indicates that all borrowed material is taken from the same source (that is, *The Dragons of Eden*), and briefly provides only what is necessary to be accurate. In such a presentation, the reader knows the source and can easily find it on the Works Cited page, as follows:

> Sagan, Carl. <u>The Dragons of Eden</u>. New York: Random, 1977.

Use endnotes or footnotes only for special purposes. Notes should *not* be used for documentation. Documentation is given by in-text citations and the complete entries on the Works Cited page. The sample research paper at the end of this chapter includes a Notes page that contains examples of some of the types of notes that are permissible.

Although notes can be useful, you should keep them to a minimum. In general, use notes only for the purposes described below.

TO INCLUDE RELEVANT BUT NON-ESSENTIAL INFORMATION

[1] Bailey discusses the many costs of maintaining a home, but he does not mention the long list of costs entailed in the initial purchase of the home. Typically, this list includes: origination fee; appraisal fee; title insurance; recording fee; survey; title exam; lien certificate. These costs often amount to a thousand dollars--and sometimes much more (<u>Home Buying</u> 26).

[2] Henning disagrees with Bernstein. He claims "nothing could relieve the economic slump" (301), but he does not elaborate.

TO LIST SUGGESTED READINGS

[3] Sheffield provides details of the meeting. Cain and O'Brien also discuss Coolidge's participation, and Martel offers a humorous but useful reminiscence.

TO GIVE DETAILS OF A PROCEDURE

[4] Subjects for testing were all ages twelve to fourteen. They were chosen for their homogenous economic background and religious affiliation.

TO PROVIDE STATISTICS

[5] Results showed that of those 18-20 years old and registered to vote, 48 percent actually voted; of those 55-64 years old, 70 percent voted.

PREPARING THE FINAL DRAFT

Follow the guidelines for manuscript form given in Manuscript Form, p. 94, when preparing the research paper for submission. In addition, careful study of the sample paper included at the end of this Part should help you with your own presentation.

In the sample paper, notes appear in a continuous list following the text of the paper and are thus correctly referred to as *endnotes*. If your instructor requires notes to appear at the bottom of pages in the text, the notes become *footnotes*. Footnotes are single-spaced instead of double-spaced, and a line is skipped between them if more than one appears on the same page. Most research papers today employ endnotes, but be sure of what is required before preparing the final draft.

PREPARING THE WORKS CITED PAGE

The Works Cited page in a research paper should include every source documented in the text of the paper and any source referred to in notes. Do *not* include sources that you examined while researching but that you did not use when writing the paper itself.

Entries are listed alphabetically by author or, if no author is listed, by the first important word of the source's title. Double-space entries and indent the second and subsequent lines of each entry five spaces. The first line of each entry should begin at the left margin.

Abbreviations

Abbreviations are used to save space, but they must be accurate enough to be unmistakable. When using an abbreviation, be sure it is accurate enough so that the reader will know — immediately and without confusion — the full version of the term. Always use a standard abbreviation, if one exists; never create abbreviations for terms that already have standard versions.

Listed here are abbreviations used in the sample Works Cited entries that follow. See the *MLA Handbook* (1984) for a complete listing of acceptable abbreviations.

dir.	directed by, director
diss.	dissertation
ed.	edited by, edition, editor
et al.	and others
GPO	Government Printing Office
rev.	revised by, revision, review
trans.	translated by, translator
vol., vols.	volume(s)
UP	University Press

Publishers' names are also abbreviated when the reader is likely to recognize the names and not be confused. For example, Harper & Row should be listed as "Harper"; Prentice-Hall, Inc. as "Prentice."

Missing data

Sometimes a source will not include the date or place of publication or the publisher's name. This is particularly true of pamphlets and documents. In such cases, the following abbreviations substitute for the missing data:

   n.p.   no place of publication given
   n.p.   no publisher given
   n.d.   no date of publication given

   <u>Auto Repair for the Amateur Mechanic</u>. n.p.: Bay

   Ridge Consumers' Council, 1980.

   <u>Caring for Patients in the Home</u>. n.p.: The East-

   mont Foundation, n.d.

Two or more works by the same author

If you cite more than one work by the same author, do not repeat the author's name in the subsequent entry. Instead, replace the author's name with three unspaced hyphens followed by a period; then list the entries alphabetically according to the first important words in the titles. For example:

   Theroux, Paul. <u>The Family Arsenal</u>. Boston:

   Houghton, 1976.

   ---. <u>Saint Jack</u>. Boston: Houghton, 1973.

Books

A BOOK WITH ONE AUTHOR

   Bronowski, J. <u>The Ascent of Man</u>. Boston: Little,

   1973.

A BOOK WITH TWO OR THREE AUTHORS

Gilson, Etienne, and Thomas Langen. Modern
   Philosophy, Descartes to Kant. New York:
   Random, 1963.

Note how only the first name listed appears in reverse order.

A BOOK WITH MORE THAN THREE AUTHORS

Alexander, Edythe, et al. Care of the Patient in
   Surgery. Saint Louis: C. V. Mosby, 1967.

A LATER EDITION

Myers, A. R. England in the Late Middle Ages.
   8th ed. Middlesex, Eng.: Penguin, 1971.

A TRANSLATION

Hesse, Hermann. Siddhartha. Trans. Hilda Rosner.
   New York: New Directions, 1951.

A WORK IN MORE THAN ONE VOLUME

Smith, Page. A New Age Now Begins. 2 vols. New
   York: McGraw, 1976.

This listing cites the entire set of a multivolume work. To cite only one volume of a multivolume work, use this form:

Smith, Page. A New Age Now Begins. 2 vols. New
   York: McGraw, 1976. Vol. 1.

A WORK ISSUED AS PART OF A SERIES

Lees, Francis Noel. <u>Gerard Manley Hopkins</u>. Columbia Essays on Modern Writers 21. New York: Columbia UP, 1966.

AN EDITED BOOK BY A SINGLE AUTHOR

Twain, Mark. <u>The Adventures of Huckleberry Finn</u>. Ed. Henry Nash Smith. Boston: Houghton, 1958.

Use this form to cite the main text of the book. To cite an introduction or preface by the editor, use the following form:

Smith, Henry Nash, ed. <u>The Adventures of Huckleberry Finn</u>. By Mark Twain. Boston: Houghton, 1958.

A SELECTION FROM AN EDITED ANTHOLOGY

Tindall, William York. "The Symbolism of W. B. Yeats." <u>Yeats: A Collection of Critical Essays</u>. Ed. John Unterecker. Englewood Cliffs: Prentice, 1963. 43-53.

The page numbers cited denote all the pages on which the selection appears in the anthology.

A SELECTION FROM A COLLECTION OF WORKS BY ONE AUTHOR

Steiner, George. "Text and Content." <u>On Difficulty</u>. Oxford: Oxford UP, 1978. 1-17.

A REPRINT

Woodberry, George E. <u>The Life of Edgar Allan Poe</u>.
2 vols. 1909. New York: Biblo and Tannen,
1965.

Include the year of original publication as shown.

Periodicals, magazines, and newspapers

A SIGNED ARTICLE IN A PERIODICAL

Fisher, Walter R. "Rationality and the Logic of
Good Reasons." <u>Philosophy and Rhetoric</u> 13
(1980): 121-130.

This entry cites volume 13. Use this form if the periodical numbers pages consecutively over the course of an entire volume. If the periodical paginates issues separately (that is, if each issue begins with page 1), use the following form:

Abrahamson, Mark, and Michael DuBick. "National
Dominance and Urban Exploitation." <u>Urban
Affairs Quarterly</u> 15.2 (1979): 146-163.

This citation denotes issue number 2 of volume 15.

A SIGNED ARTICLE IN A MAGAZINE

Kennen, George. "America's Unstable Soviet Policy."
<u>Atlantic</u> Nov. 1982: 71-80.

If the magazine appears weekly, include the full date of the issue:

Caraganis, Lynn. "Surge in Church Attendance, Tri-State Area." <u>New Yorker</u> 1 Nov. 1982: 38-39.

AN UNSIGNED ARTICLE IN A MAGAZINE

"Carter's Plan: Criticized, but Flexible." <u>Time</u> 24 Jan. 1977: 45-46.

A REVIEW

Raban, Jonathan. "Innocents Abroad." Rev. of <u>Monsignor Quixote</u>, by Graham Greene. <u>New York Review of Books</u> 4 Nov. 1982: 18+.

The plus symbol (+) denotes the fact that the review appears on more than one page but not on consecutive pages. Use the plus symbol this way in any entry where it is appropriate.

A SIGNED ARTICLE IN A NEWSPAPER

Bernstein, Richard. "Nuclear Foes Ponder Fate of the Earth." <u>New York Times</u> 22 Oct. 1982: B1+.

This citation identifies an article in section B of an issue in which each separate section begins with page 1. If sections are not paginated in this way, cite only the page number(s).

AN UNSIGNED ARTICLE IN A NEWSPAPER

"MX Basing Plan Reportedly Outlined." <u>Boston Globe</u> 20 Aug. 1982: 9.

Other sources

A SIGNED ARTICLE IN AN ENCYCLOPEDIA

Hayward, John T. "Guided Missiles." <u>Encyclopedia Americana</u>. 1982 ed.

Volume, page numbers, and publication data are not required for well-known encyclopedias, annuals, or yearbooks that arrange information alphabetically.

An Unsigned Article in an Encyclopedia

"Sir Thomas More." New Columbia Encyclopedia. 1975 ed.

Bulletins, Pamphlets, and Government Publications

American Public Opinion and U.S. Foreign Policy 1979. Chicago: Chicago Council on Foreign Relations, 1979.

United States. Dept. of Health and Human Services. Blood Transfusions: Benefits and Risks. Washington: GPO, 1981.

Unpublished Dissertations and Theses

Foley, Jessica. "Parenting and Public Policy: An Historical Overview." Diss. U of Massachusetts, 1972.

Films and Television Programs

Hackford, Taylor, dir. An Officer and A Gentleman. Paramount, 1982.

"Amate: The Great Fig Tree." Nature. WGBH, Boston. 31 Oct. 1982.

Exercise   205

RECORDS

Dylan, Bob. <u>Blood on the Tracks</u>. Columbia,
  PC 33235, 1974.

To cite a specific song on an album, use this form:

Dylan, Bob. "Meet Me in the Morning." <u>Blood on
  the Tracks</u>. Columbia, PC 33235, 1974.

To cite jacket notes, use this form, citing the author of the notes:

Hamill, Pete. Jacket notes. <u>Blood on the Tracks</u>.
  Columbia, PC 33235, 1974.

INTERVIEWS

Perkins, C. E. Personal interview. 3 Feb. 1979.

Matte, Cynthia. Telephone interview. 16 May 1983.

EXERCISE

Below is information on sources that might appear in a research paper. Construct a Works Cited page for the same sources. Inclusive page numbers for articles are given in brackets.

1. A book published in 1968 by the Viking Press in New York. Title: Doctor Johnson and His World. Author: F. E. Halliday.
2. An article in the magazine Discover. Page 12 of the January 1983 issue. No author listed. Title of article: Story of the Rings. [11–12]

3. A book published in Baltimore by the Johns Hopkins University Press in 1979. Author: Marcel Detienne. Title: Dionysos Slain. Translated by Mireille Muellner and Leonard Muellner.
4. An article in an edited anthology. Title of anthology: Class and Society in Early America. Title of article: Social Stratification. Author of article: Bernard Barber. Editor of anthology: Gary B. Nash. Published in 1970 by Prentice-Hall, Inc., Englewood Cliffs, N. J. [75–89]
5. Volume I of a two-volume work titled The Americans. Publisher: Capricorn Books in New York. Year: 1969. Author: J. C. Furnas.
6. An unsigned newspaper article in the January 19, 1983 issue of The Boston Globe. Title: Unfit-Parent Ruling Is Upheld by Court. [21].
7. A book published in 1972 in New York. Authors: Orville Schell and Joseph Esherick. Publisher: Random House. Title: Modern China.
8. A periodical article in volume III, issue number 3, of The Kenyon Review. Author: Robert Langbaum. Title: Freud and Sociobiology: Reflections on the Nature of Genius. 1981. [105–120]
9. A reprint of a book originally published in 1841. Publisher: Harmony Books in New York. Author: Charles Mackay. Title: Extraordinary Popular Delusions and the Madness of Crowds. Reprint published in 1980.
10. An article in a collection of Lionel Trilling's essays. Title of collection: Beyond Culture. Title of essay: The Fate of Pleasure. Published in 1979 in New York by Harcourt Brace Jovanovich. [50–76]

A SAMPLE RESEARCH PAPER

Nathaniel Copley's research paper, which follows, adheres to the guidelines given in this Part. As a sample, it is intended to help you see how your own papers should be constructed and presented. He has followed the style for notes and the Works Cited page given

A Sample Research Paper 207

in the *MLA Handbook*. Commentary appears on left-hand pages to highlight and explain the many details that need attention when any research paper is written and typed. Numbers in the body of the paper correspond to the numbers given in the commentary. To derive the greatest benefit, you should pay close attention not only to *what* the paper says but also to *how* Nathaniel has completed his assignment.

The title page should contain at least the research paper's title and your own name. Other information can be included as your instructor directs, but be sure to create a balanced look on the page.

1. When typing the paper's title, use upper and lower case letters. Do not use quotation marks, underlining, or any other such device.

Watching the Blinking Light: A New

Attitude Toward Death and Dying

By

Nathaniel Copley

English 101, Section 215

Mr. Simpson

March 15, 198-

2. If you include an outline with the research paper, place it after the title page and before the first page of text. Do not number the outline's first page; number any subsequent pages using lowercase Roman numerals (ii, iii, etc.).

Watching the Blinking Light: A New
Attitude Toward Death and Dying

Thesis: Never before has our society made a meaningful effort to understand the process of dying, but because we are now making such an effort, we are replacing ignorance with understanding and fear with acceptance.

I. The first step toward understanding has been to overcome resistance to discussing the subject.
    A. Death has been a "taboo topic."
    B. Dying is now viewed as a process in which others can participate and offer comfort.

II. This first step is being prompted by medical advances.
    A. Technology is prolonging life.
    B. Technology is affecting the definition of "death."

C. Health professionals are changing their own attitude toward death and dying.

III. We can find many manifestations of the changing attitude.

    A. The hospice movement is the most obvious manifestation.

    B. Society is also making efforts to finance care for the dying.

    C. Laws are adjusting to make a place for the dying.

        1. The living will has been created.

        2. Many states are considering "Right-to-Die" laws.

IV. Society has not resolved all the issues raised by our new attitude toward death and dying, but it now finally acknowledges them.

3   The title is centered. It is also double-spaced here because its length requires two lines. Four spaces follow before the text begins. This first page is not numbered; a number would be unnecessary because the presence of the paper's title clearly identifies this as the first page.

4   Paragraph 1 serves as a lead-in and accomplishes two goals. It captures the reader's attention by posing a question. Furthermore, it helps avoid an abrupt beginning. The author wastes no time in moving toward his thesis (which is contained in paragraph 2), but he does not leap into the thesis, a move that might be mechanically acceptable but stylistically unpleasant. Note also how the author has most likely drawn on his own experience (viewing the museum display), but he avoids using the first person "I." Using the first person would be inconsistent because nowhere else in the paper does the author use it.

5   The quotation from *Hamlet* is not documented because within the context of this paper doing so would serve no purpose. The audience should be familiar with the play. The paper also is not about *Hamlet*. By quoting a popular seventeenth century source, the author is reinforcing his statement that fear of death is not new and has affected everyone.

Watching the Blinking Light: A New
Attitude Toward Death and Dying

A museum in a large city presents a display aimed at explaining world population. The display includes graphs and charts showing trends in population over the centuries, and it also includes a board on which appear two lights. One light flashes to mark the birth of each new person; the other light flashes each time a human being dies. Both lights flash often, the birth light more often than the other, and the discrepancy is meant to show how fast the earth's population is increasing. Studying the slower light, however, the "death light," should make anyone pause. The birth light might blink more quickly, but what about the other light?

Answering this question reveals just how far we have come in addressing the problems death presents for us. We have always feared death, what Hamlet called "The undiscover'd country from whose bourn/ No traveler returns," and we have sought to avoid

6 Page 2 is the first page to be numbered. The page number appears in the upper right-hand corner far enough from the text to avoid confusion with note numbers.

7 The author states his thesis. The next sentence ("Sudden, unexpected death . . . .") serves to limit the topic further.

8 The author documents the term "taboo topic" because it is not a term of his own devising. Note also how in this paragraph (and everywhere else in the paper), the author smoothly incorporates quoted material, using the ellipsis as necessary to maintain the integrity of original sources while composing complete, readable sentences.

the subject whenever possible. This attitude, however, is changing. Never before has our society made a meaningful effort to understand the process of dying, but because we are now making such an effort, we are replacing ignorance with understanding and fear with acceptance. Sudden, unexpected death will always shock those who are left behind and will always present problems that are probably beyond solving completely, but when death approaches slowly and deliberately, our reaction, we are discovering, can be controlled and helpful.

The first step toward understanding death and dying is to overcome resistance to discussing the subject. Death has been called "a taboo topic," as Vanderlyn R. Pine has pointed out (322). We all feel a reluctance to address the issue, and this reluctance has affected doctors and other health professionals as well. The psychological and cultural reasons for the taboo are varied and sometimes seem contradictory, but the barriers are beginning

9   The paragraph begins with a transition echoing the first sentence of the preceding paragraph. This links the two paragraphs, which is appropriate considering the points the author is making.

3

to fall. The first step in the change has been brought about by a new willingness to explore just what death is. "Death is often treated as an event in time and space. . . ," as Pine says, but "from the social perspective, death, too, is a process which occurs over time" (320). The word "process" appears repeatedly in all the new discussions of death, and its use is essential. A process has steps or stages, and unlike an "event," it presents the possibility of participation. We can play a role in a process. We are mere spectators at an event. Such a distinction is at the core of the attitude we are beginning to adopt.

This first step toward understanding is being prompted in part by medical advances. Technology today is prolonging the lives of people who in past years would not have survived, and we are being forced to re-examine our definition of death itself. Just when is a person dead? This question seemed superfluous a hundred years ago, but today we cannot

10 A triple-space appears before and after the quotation. The quotation is indented ten spaces and is double-spaced. Use this form with any quotation that would occupy more than four lines of text if it were double-spaced and not indented. Do not use quotation marks around a long quotation (unless they appear in the original). Quotation marks serve to separate your words from those of others, and when a quotation is indented and double-spaced, the separation is obvious. For more discussion of this point, see Uses of Quotation Marks, pp. 117–121.

  4

be sure how to answer. In Death, Dying, and the

Biological Revolution, Robert M. Veatch notes that

defining death today presents ethical as well as

technical problems. The problems overlap, and easy

answers are impossible. We must, in effect, define

what life is so as to define death, and "To ask what

is essentially significant to a human being is a

philosophical question--a question of ethical and

other values" (29). We are, however, starting to

ask the question.

Health professionals, doctors, nurses, coun-

selors, and others who work with the dying are par-

ticularly aware of the need to review our attitude.

The "Front-Line Physician," as John M. Flexner

calls him, can bring science into play, but more

is needed. Flexner offers a concise summary:

   Science deals with treating the patient's   10
   illness in an up-to-date fashion through
   present knowledge, protocols, and methods.
   The Humanitarian approach deals pri-

11   The author is summarizing material contained in three pages of the original source.

12   Nathaniel reaffirms his thesis at this point, thus keeping his main idea squarely before the audience. Doing so at this point is convenient because the author is concluding one section of his argument before moving on to the next section.

13   A problem exists at this point. The author says that Dubois cites research, clearly implying that the author is getting his information second-hand (from a secondary source). Doing so is often dangerous, and the author would be much safer if he located Dubois' sources and cited them (the primary sources) rather than Dubois.

marily with the patient's problems of adjusting to his illness and its therapy. This may be termed the personal aspect of care-giving. Here we are using "The Art" as opposed to "The Science" (172).

Flexner goes on to state that the physician must be part of a "care-giving team" composed of many members: nurses, ward technicians, chaplains, family members, psychiatrists, social workers, friends, and also philosophers and lawyers (180-182). Today such teams are being assembled. The "Art" of health care is opening up to the terminally ill, and the changes are designed not only to ease anxiety but to make a place for death and dying in our society, something we have never done or have done only reluctantly.

The most obvious manifestation of our changing attitude is the hospice, a home specifically designed to care for the physical and psychological needs of the dying. The hospice concept is not new. In The Hospice Way of Death, Paul M. Dubois cites

14 A summary. The original appears as follows:

"Three other physical aspects of the early hospices are noteworthy. First, there was a pharmacy in the hospice available to inpatients and outpatients and usable by all citizens of the town. Second, the hospice was located in the very center of the town, immediately adjacent to the marketplace, so that accessibility of visitors and customers to the pharmacy was easy. Third, there was a peaceful, charming, even beautiful courtyard within the hospice walls, a place in which patients undoubtedly found quiet and solace."

15 In this and the next two paragraphs, the author does not name the sources in the text of the paper. He is merely taking information, and naming the sources in the text would serve no purpose, would take up space unnecessarily, and would soon become cumbersome and interfere with the flow of ideas.

16 The Hotchkiss article appears on only one page. Hence, no page number is documented.

6

research showing that the first hospices were "early Christian hospitals set up to care for all unfortunates, orphans, the aged, the sick, and wayfarers travelling between cities or to holy places on pilgrimages" (60). In them, "medical management, comfort, and spiritual care . . . were the primary objectives" (60). These early hospices also provided a pharmacy for patients and all citizens of the town, were centrally located for easy access, and included a peaceful courtyard (61).

This emphasis on both body and mind exists today in the modern hospice movement, which began in London with the institution of St. Christopher's Hospice in 1967. Today over thirty hospices operate in England, and the movement has spread to North America where hospice care is sometimes hospital-based or provided in the home as well as in institutions dedicated solely to care for the dying (Davidson 158-168). Some programs depend primarily on volunteer effort, as in the Shanti project in San Francisco (Hotchkiss), and some rely on full-

time professionals such as those at the Hillhaven Hospice in Tucson, Arizona (Davidson 167).

No matter where hospice services are provided or who provides them, the care differs from that which a hospital can offer. Physical symptoms must be addressed, but the hospice concept includes other elements, among them:

>--reasonable fulfillment of individual lifestyles
>--the incorporation of family members into the decision-making process, even when special education may be required
>--continuing follow-up for the bereaved
>--a physical design that permits independence of movement, privacy, and community
>--the integration of children into the life of the hospice
>--considerable interaction among the dying (Dubois 65-66).

17 The author once again reaffirms his thesis.

Some hospices use the creative arts to help the terminally ill. Keeping a journal, writing poetry, working at crafts, and other "creative communications" can do much to relieve stress and alleviate the feeling of abandonment that impending death creates (Rogers 123). All these elements help distinguish the hospice from the traditional hospital. The psychological effects of the death process receive as much attention as the physical. Emphasis is on the whole person.

The hospice movement may be the most obvious sign that our society is changing its attitude toward the dying, but hospice care presents one problem. It can be costly, and this cost is a new factor. Traditional medical care is aimed at restoring health, and insurance plans are designed to provide funds to serve this purpose. How then can the goal of hospice care, which is not to "restore" irretrievably lost health, be reconciled with the demands of insurance coverage? Response

18–
19   The Works Cited entries for these sources list no authors. Documentation thus calls for providing short versions of the articles' titles. Another example of this method appears in the next paragraph.

to this problem shows tentative signs that here, too, our society is beginning to make a place for the dying. In April 1980, The Health Care Financing Administration of the Department of Health, Education, and Welfare announced a two-year project in which Medicare and Medicaid patients at twenty-six selected hospices around the country would have all their expenses paid ("Supporting" 160). Another similar step is the move by Blue Cross-Blue Shield (the predominant health care insurer in the northeastern United States) to cover almost unlimited home care for dying patients who forgo hospital treatment. The insurer also intends to extend hospice coverage, although nursing home care is not covered and still presents a problem ("Care" 4). These policy changes by Medicare and Medicaid and Blue Cross-Blue Shield, two of the country's largest providers of health care coverage, indicate the direction for the future.

    Another manifestation of the changing attitude

is the living will. In <u>The Right to Die with Dignity</u>, Elizabeth Ogg defines the living will as:

> . . . a document you can sign at any time of your adult life while you are "of sound mind." It enables you to direct, if you wish, that should you become terminally ill, no "heroic" medical techniques are to be used to prolong your life. . . . The two-fold purpose of a living will is, first, to ensure that your wishes as to treatment during terminal illness will be known even if you become comatose or incompetent; and, second, to protect health care professionals from charges of malpractice by providing, in advance, your written, informed consent to the withholding or withdrawing of life-prolonging technology (7).

The living will is part of a larger effort to

20 The author is paraphrasing. The original appears as follows: "The major responsibility for deciding what should or should not be done for dying patients has traditionally belonged to hospital-based doctors. Now there is a movement afoot to enable others — patients, their families, and patients' representatives — to have a say in such decisions."

21 This paragraph is purely transitional. It prepares the way for the conclusion that follows.

re-examine what should be done for the dying. As
Ogg says, most decisions in this matter have traditionally been made by hospital-based doctors, but
a movement is growing to enable others (patients,
their families, and patients' representatives) to
participate in making these decisions (3). Right-to-Die laws are another part of this effort. The
main purpose of such laws is to give legal weight
to living wills, and at least ten states have
enacted pertinent legislation. Such laws remain
controversial; the Massachusetts legislature, for
example, debated the living will for five years
before making any headway toward passing legislation,
and final enactment is still uncertain ("Living
Will"). Public discussion of Right-to-Die laws will
undoubtedly continue, but the movement is strong to
make laws adapt to the new attitude toward death
and dying.

Public discussion, however, centers on public
issues. What about people--the people on whom
this discussion focuses?

22 The author reviews his entire presentation in the conclusion, but he avoids mechanically restating his thesis. He also avoids an abrupt ending, which would be just as unpleasant as an abrupt beginning.

23 Notes 1, 2, and 3 allow the author to include related material in his research paper, but without slowing down his presentation.

24 The author returns to the anecdote he uses in the introduction, thus coming full circle.

12

A nurse who works daily with terminal patients in a Boston hospital perhaps best summarizes the feelings of those most directly affected by the new attitude: "I'm glad we can at least talk about this subject now. The dying need us all" (Tremain). Our willingness to talk has indeed increased. Works such as <u>On Death and Dying</u> by well-known researcher Elizabeth Kübler-Ross[1] can be found in even the most limited libraries. Popular magazines feature articles on the formerly hidden topic,[2] and some educators believe that the topic will eventually be included in school curricula.[3] All this open discussion accompanies our tangible efforts at providing care and sorting out the financial and legal ramifications of the new attitude toward death and dying. Although society has not yet resolved all the issues, it now finally acknowledges them. We have begun to watch the museum's blinking light.

25 Center the heading, skip four lines, and begin listing notes. Double-space endnote entries, indenting five spaces for only the first line of each entry.

26– The information in note 2 offers examples to substantiate what
27 the author has claimed in the text of his paper. The examples are carefully chosen. The author has said that popular magazines have discussed the topic, so in the note he has listed magazines that do not appeal to limited, specialized audiences. Note 3 directs the audience to a source that might prove useful if a reader wishes to pursue a particular subject. In the case of both notes, the author has chosen not to include the information in the text because the information would interfere with the flow of ideas. The information *is* valuable, however, so the author has chosen the notes as the most appropriate place to present it.

Notes

[1] Kübler-Ross' public prominence is itself another indication of the new attitude.

[2] See as examples: Alice Lake's "A Chance to Say Goodbye," McCall's, Feb. 1982; "Death in America: No Longer a Hidden Subject," U.S. News & World Report, 13 Nov. 1978; "Living with Dying," Newsweek, 1 May 1978.

[3] For extensive discussion of this subject, see: Richard O. Ulin, Death and Dying Education.

28   Center the heading, skip four lines, and begin listing entries. Double-space entries, indenting all lines five spaces except the first line of each entry, which begins at the left margin.

29   An unsigned periodical article. Note how the author has listed the page number as "1+." The article in question begins on page one and is continued on page four where it ends. Using the plus symbol (+) indicates that the article is continued on non-consecutive pages.

30   An article in an edited anthology.

31   A book by one author.

32   A signed magazine article.

Works Cited

"Care for the Dying: Insurer and Provider Discuss the Issues." <u>Concern for Dying</u> 6.2 (1980): 1+.

Davidson, Glen W. "Hospice Care for the Dying." <u>Dying: Facing the Facts</u>. Ed. Hannelore Wass. Washington: Hemisphere, 1979. 158-181.

"Death in America: No Longer a Hidden Subject." <u>U.S. News & World Report</u> 13 Nov. 1978: 67-68+.

Dubois, Paul M. <u>The Hospice Way of Death</u>. New York: Human Sciences, 1980.

Flexner, John M. "Dying, Death, and the 'Front-Line Physician.'" <u>Dying and Death: A Clinical Guide for Caregivers</u>. Ed. David Barton. Baltimore: Williams & Wilkins, 1977. 170-182.

Hotchkiss, Sandy. "Peaceful Dying, A Humane Approach to the Terminally Ill." <u>Human Behavior</u> April 1978: 32.

Kübler-Ross, Elizabeth. <u>On Death and Dying</u>. New York: Macmillan, 1969.

33   An unsigned newspaper article.

34   An article in an edited anthology. The anthology names four editors, but only the first is listed, followed by "et al." ("and others").

35   An unsigned magazine article.

Lake, Alice. "A Chance to Say Goodbye." McCall's
    Feb. 1982: 60+.

"Living Will Passes in House." Lowell Sun 18 May
    1982: 16.

"Living with Dying." Newsweek 1 May 1978: 53-56+.

Ogg, Elizabeth. The Right to Die with Dignity.
    New York: Public Affairs Committee, 1980.

Pine, Vanderlyn R. "Communicating Issues in
    Thanatology: The State of the Art." Communi-
    cating Issues in Thanatology. Ed. Thomas J.
    Fleming, et al. New York: MSS Information
    Corp., 1976. 319-328.

Rogers, Barry LeGrove. "Using the Creative Process
    with the Terminally Ill." The Hospice:
    Development and Administration. Ed. Glen W.
    Davidson. Washington: Hemisphere, 1978.
    123-126.

"Supporting Hospice Care." Science 11 Jan. 1980:
    160-161.

Tremain, Florence. Telephone interview. 16 March
    1982.

16

Ulin, Richard O. <u>Death and Dying Education</u>.
Washington: National Education Association,
1977.

Veatch, Robert M. <u>Death, Dying, and the Biological
Revolution</u>. New Haven: Yale UP, 1976.

1923, © 1969 by Holt, Rinehart and Winston. Copyright 1951 by Robert Frost. Reprinted by permission of Holt, Rinehart and Winston, Publishers, the Estate of Robert Frost, and Jonathan Cape Ltd.

Pages 128, 137–138. Excerpts from *The Autobiography of Lincoln Steffens*. Copyright 1931 by Harcourt Brace Jovanovich, Inc.; renewed 1959 by Peter Steffens. Reprinted by permission of the publisher.

Pages 139, 140. Excerpts from "Street Haunting" in *The Death of the Moth and Other Essays* by Virginia Woolf, © 1942 by Harcourt Brace Jovanovich, Inc.; renewed 1970 by Marjorie T. Parsons, Executrix. Reprinted by permission of Harcourt Brace Jovanovich, Inc., the Author's Literary Estate, and the Hogarth Press Ltd.

Index

Abbreviations, 41–45
  capitalization of, 62
  courses of instruction, 44
  days, months, and holidays, 44
  dollars, cents, and percentages, 44
  foreign phrases, standard, 43
  geographical names, 44
  List of Works Cited, 198
  organizations, 42–43
  technical terms, 42
  time, 42
  titles and degrees, 41–42
  unacceptable abbreviations, 43–44
Absolute phrases, 36
accept, except, 163
Active voice, 12, 140–142, 173
Addresses, 97, 106
Ad hominem, 90
Adjective clause, 37–38
Adjectives, 24–26
  and adverbs, 45–48
  comparative, 25, 46–48
  coordinating, 103–104
  irregular, 25–26, 47–48
  after linking verbs, 46
  negative comparisons, 47
  position in sentence, 45
  positive, 25, 47–48
  superlative, 25, 46–48
Adverb clause, 38
Adverbials, 24
Adverbs, 26–27
  and adjectives, 45–48
  comparative, 46–48
  conjunctive, 28–29, 65
  irregular, 47–48
  limiting, 92
  negative comparisons, 47
  of place, time, manner, or degree, 45–46
  positive, 47–48
  superlative, 46–48
affect, effect, 163
Agreement of pronoun and antecedent, 21, 144–147
  with collective nouns, 52
  compound antecedents, 143
  indefinite pronouns, 143–144
  in model essay, 13–14.
  See also Pronouns
Agreement of subject and verb, 49–53
  with collective nouns, 52
  with compound subjects, 50–51
  with indefinite pronouns, 51
  with linking verbs, 53
  with nouns of time, money, weight, and measurement, 53
  with relative pronouns, 53
  with titles, 53
all ready, already, 164
all right, alright, 164
allusion, illusion, 163
already, all ready, 164

alright, all right, 164
Ambiguous (squinting) modifiers, 93
among, between, 164
Analogy
   false, 90
   in paragraph development, 135
angry at, angry with, 73
Antecedents
   of collective nouns, 52
   indefinite pronouns, 143
   of pronouns, 21, 144–147
Apostrophe, 121–124
   definition, 121
   with contractions, 123
   with plural letters and numbers, 123
   with possessive case, 121–122
Appositives
   definition, 57
   with colon, 112
   with comma, 105–106
Articles, 30
as, 57
as, like, 167
as or *than,* 57
Audience, 3, 5–6
Auxiliary verbs, 23, 36

bad, badly, 164
beside, besides, 164
best, better, 164
between, among, 164
Biblical citations, 113
Bibliography, working, 180–181. *See also* List of Works Cited
Brackets, 116

can, may, 164
Capitalization, 59–63
   abbreviations, 62
   directions, 62–63
   historical events, periods, and documents, 60
   names of organizations, departments, 60
   political and social groups, 60
   proper nouns and adjectives, 59–60
   races, nationalities, and languages, 60
   relations, 61–62
   religious names, 60–61
   school courses, 61
   titles of books, 59
   titles of persons, 61
   trade names, 62
Card catalogue, 181
Case, 54–58
   appositives, 57
   compound constructions, 56
   definition, 54
   objective, 55
   possessive, 55–56
   of pronouns, 21–22
   subjective, 54–55
   using *than* or *as,* 57
   using *we* or *us,* 56–57
   using *who* or *whom,* 57–58
Cause and effect, 135
cite, site, 165
Clauses, 36–38
   adjective, 37–38
   adverb, 38
   dependent, 22, 38–39
   independent, 37
   noun, 37
Clichés, 64–65
   common, 64–65
   definition, 64
Coherence (of paragraphs), 131–133
Collective nouns, 52
Colloquial language, 72
Colon, 112–113
   in biblical citations, 113
   in divisions of time, 113
   with explanations, 112–113
   in formal letters, 113
   with formal quotations, 112

Index

with list of appositives, 112
with titles and subtitles, 113
Comma, 102–108
  with absolute phrases, 107
  with coordinating adjectives, 103–105
  with dates, addresses, 107
  with independent clauses, 102–103
  with introductory elements, 104
  with items in a series, 103
  with nonrestrictive modifiers and appositives, 105–106
  with parenthetical elements and transitional words, 106–107
  with quotations, 108
Comma splices, 68–69
Comparative adjectives, 25
Comparison and contrast, 135
complement, compliment, 165
Complements
  direct object, 33
  indirect object, 33–34
  subject, 34
Complex sentences, 38
compliment, complement, 165
Compound-complex sentences, 39
Compound sentences, 38
Concluding paragraphs, 15, 138–139
Conjunctions, 28–30
  conjunctive adverbs, 28–29
  coordinating, 65, 98
  correlative, 28
  subordinating, 29–30
Conjunctive adverbs, 28–29, 65
Connotation, 74–75
continuous, continual, 165
Coordinate adjectives, 103
Coordinating adjectives, 103–104
Coordinating conjunctions, 28, 65, 98

Coordination
  conjunctive adverbs, 65
  coordinating conjunctions, 65
  faulty, 65–67
Correlative conjunctions, 28

Dangling modifiers, 76–77
Dash, 113–115
  with interruptions and parenthetic elements, 114
  with introductory substantives, 114–115
  with nonrestrictive elements, 114
  with summary statements, 114
Dates, 44, 97, 107
Declarative sentences, 32
Demonstrative pronouns, 22
Denotation, 74–75
Dependent clause, 22, 37–38
Details, 133–136
Determiners, 30
Diction, 70–76
  colloquial language, 72
  conciseness, 75
  current and general use, 71
  denotation and connotation, 74–75
  idioms, 72–73
  in model essay, 14
  regionalisms, 71
  slang, 72
  technical words, 71–72
different from, different than, 73
differ from, differ with, 165
Direct object, 33
Direct quotation, 117–118
  with commas, 108
  with other marks of punctuation, 120
  quotation marks for, 100–101, 117–119
disinterested, uninterested, 165–166
Documentation, 190–197
  by title, 193–194

Documentation [*cont.*]
  endnotes and footnotes, 196–197
  List of Works Cited, 191–194, 198–205
  more than one source, 195
  of multivolume work, 194–195
  of work by two or three authors, 192
  of work by three or more authors, 192–193
  See also List of Works Cited
due to the fact that, 166

effect, affect, 163
Ellipsis mark, 124–125
Emphasis
  dashes for, 113–115
  exclamation point for, 101–102
Endnotes. *See* Documentation, and List of Works Cited
English, standard and nonstandard. *See* Standard American English
except, accept, 163
Exclamation point, 101–102
Expletives, 32
explicit, implicit, 166

False analogy, 90
farther, further, 166
Faulty coordination, 65–67
Faulty logic, 88–91
  ad hominem, 90
  false analogy, 90
  hasty generalization, 88–89
  immoderate tone, 88
  non sequitur, 89–90
  oversimplification, 88
  post hoc, 89
  stereotypes, 90
Faulty parallelism, 97–99
Figures. *See* Numbers
Footnotes. *See* Documentation, and List of Works Cited

Foreign plurals, 151–152
Formal outline, 188–190
Fragments. *See* Sentence fragments
further, farther, 166
Fused sentences, 82–83

Geographical names
  abbreviations, 44
  capitalization, 59–60
  commas with, 107
Gerund phrase, 35
good, well, 166

hanged, hung, 166–167
Helping verbs, 23, 36
hyphens, 83–85
  for compound expressions, 84
  in fractions and compound numbers, 84
  in model essay, 12
  for preventing ambiguity, 85
  for word divisions, 84

Idioms, 72–73
illusion, allusion, 163
Imperative sentences, 33
implicit, explicit, 166
imply, infer, 167
Indefinite pronouns, 22, 51
  agreement of, 143–144
Independent clause, 22, 37
  with comma, 102–103
  with semicolon, 109–110
Indirect object, 33–34
Indirect quotation, 118
infer, imply, 167
Infinitive phrase, 35–36
Inflectional endings, 19
Informal (colloquial) Standard American English, 71–72
Intensive pronouns, 22
Interjections, 30–31
Interrogative pronouns, 22
Interrogative sentences, 32–33
Intransitive verbs, 24

Index

Introductory paragraphs, 3, 137–138
irregardless, 167
Irregular adjectives, 25–26
Irregular verbs, 23
Italics, 85–87
  for emphasis, 87
  for foreign words and phrases, 86
  for names of vehicles, 86
  for titles, 85–86
  underlining to indicate italics, 85
  for words, numbers, and figures, 87

Language, appropriate. *See* Diction
lay, lie, 167
like, as, 167
Linking verbs, 24
List of Works Cited, 198–202
  abbreviations, 198
  books, 199–200
  definition, 198
  missing data, 199
  from model research paper, 241, 243, 245
  other sources, 203–205
  periodicals: magazines and newspapers, 202–203
  two or more works by same author, 199
Logic. *See* Faulty logic

Main clauses. *See* Independent clauses
Main verbs, 36
Manuscript form, 94–96
  handwritten papers, 95
  proofreading and corrections, 95–96
  typed papers, 94
may, can, 164–165
Misplaced modifier, 13, 91–93
  ambiguous (squinting) modifiers, 93

limiting adverbs, 92
prepositional phrases and subordinate clauses, 92
Model essays, 7–18
  "The Birth of an Outdoorsman," 15–18
  "Garfield is a Star," 8–10
Modern Language Association 1984 Documentation guidelines, 177, 198
Modifiers
  ambiguous, 93
  dangling, 76–77
  limiting adverbs, 92
  misplaced, 13, 91–93
  prepositional phrases and subordinate clauses, 92
  squinting, 93

Nonrestrictive modifiers, 13
Non sequitur, 89
Nonstandard English, 70–72
Note cards, 180
Notes, 185–187
  direct quotations, 185
  paraphrasing, 185–186
  summary, 186–187
Noun clauses, 37
Noun phrases, 36
Nouns, 20
  collective, 52
  proper, 20
Numbers, use of, 96–97

Object complement, 34
Objective case, 21
Objects
  direct, 33
  indirect, 33–34
  of prepositions, 34–35
Opening sentences, 137–138
Organizations, names of, 60
Outline
  formal outline, 4, 188–190
  prewriting, 3–5
  "scratch" (random) outline, 4
  sentence outline, 188–189

Outline [*cont.*]
   tentative outline for research paper, 183–184
   topic outline, 188–189

Pamphlet and document files, 182
Paragraphs, 127–140
   coherence of, 131–133. *See also* Transitions
   concluding, 138–140
   development of, 133–137
   introductory, 3, 137–138
   supporting detail, 134–136
   topic sentence in, 127–129, 133–136
   transitional, 127. *See also* Transitions
   unity of, 127–130
Parallel structure, 97–99, 131
Parentheses, 115–117
Participial phrases, 13, 35
Parts of a sentence, 31–39
Parts of speech, 19–31
Passive voice, 12, 14, 140–142, 173
Past perfect tense. *See* Verbs
Past tense. *See* Verbs
Period, 99–100
   with abbreviations, 99–100
   with commands and indirect questions, 99
   with ellipsis mark, 124
   at end of sentence, 99
   with quotation marks, 100
   unnecessary uses of, 100
Periodical indexes, 181–182
Personal pronouns, 21
Phrases, 34–36
   absolute, 36
   gerund, 35
   infinitive, 35–36
   noun, 36
   participial, 35
   prepositional, 34–35
   verb, 36
   verbal, 35

Plagiarism, 187–188
Positive degree of adjectives, 25
Post hoc, 89
Predicate adjectives, 34
Predicate nouns, 34
Predicates, 33–34
Prepositional phrases, 2, 7, 34–35, 92
Prepositions, 27–28
Present perfect tense. *See* Verbs
Present tense. *See* Verbs
Pretentious language, avoiding, 71
Prewriting, 1–6
   audience, 3, 5
   checklist, 6
   formal outline, 4
   introductory paragraph, 3
   outline, 3–5
   purpose, 3, 5
   "scratch" (random) outline, 4
   thesis, 2
   thesis sentence, 2
   topic, 2
Primary sources, 182
Principal parts of verbs, 23
principal, principle, 167–168
Pronouns, 21–22, 142–147
   antecedent, 21, 142–147
   demonstrative, 22
   errors in reference and agreement, 142–147
   indefinite, 22
   intensive, 22
   interrogative, 22
   reference of, 13–14, 144–147
   relative pronouns, 22
Proper nouns, 20

Question mark, 100–101
   with direct questions, 100
   with parenthesis, 101
   with quotation marks, 101
Quotation marks, 117–120
   for dialogue, 118
   direct quotations, 117–118
   lengthy passages, 118–119

Index

with other marks of punctuation, 120
for poetry, 118–119
for quotations within quotations, 119
with titles, 119
with words in special sense, 119
quotation, quote, 168

raise, rise, 168
Redundant phrases, avoiding, 174
Reference of pronouns. *See* Pronouns
Reflexive pronouns, 21
Relative pronouns, 22
Repetition
    avoiding unnecessary, 172–175
    for emphasis, 174
    redundant phrases, 174
Research paper, 177–205
    avoiding plagiarism, 187–188
    card catalogue, 181–182
    defined, 177–180
    final draft, 197
    first draft, 190–197
    formal outline, 188–190
    List of Works Cited, 198–205
    methods of documentation, 190–197
    model research paper, 209–245
    note cards, 180–181
    notes for, 185–187
    pamphlet and document files, 182
    periodical indexes, 181–182
    primary sources, 182
    researching the topic, 180–186
    secondary sources, 183
    tentative outline, 183–184
    tentative thesis, 183–184
    working bibliography, 180–181
rise, raise, 168
Run-on sentences, 82–83

Secondary sources, 183
Semicolon, 109–111
    with conjunctive adverbs, 110
    with independent clauses, 109–110
    with items in a series, 110–111
    with long and complex clauses, 110
sensual, sensuous, 168
Sentences, 31–39
    commands, 33
    complex, 38
    compound, 38
    compound-complex, 39
    declarative, 32
    fragments, 78–82
    imperative, 33
    interrogative, 32–33
    kinds of, 38–39
    opening, 137–138
    questions, 32–33
    simple, 38
    structure in model essay, 12–13
    variety, 169–171
set, sit, 168 ← Sexist language 143
sic, 116–117
Simple sentences, 38
site, cite, 164
Slang, 72
Slash, 125
Sources, 181–183
    acknowledging, 187–188, 198–205
    card catalogue, 181
    List of Works Cited, 198–205
    periodical indexes, 181–182
    pamphlet and documentation, 182
    primary, 182
    secondary, 183
    working bibliography, 180–181
Spelling, 147–153
Spelling rules, 148–149
Squinting modifiers, 93

Standard American English, 70–76
Stereotypes, 90
Subject complement, 34
Subjects
  agreement of verb with, 49–53
  compound, 50–51
  of sentences, 32–33
Subordinate clauses, 36–38
Subordinating conjunctions, 29–30, 154–156
Subordination, 153–156
Superlative adjectives, 25

Technical terms, avoiding, 71
Tense, 23
than, 57
than or *as,* 57
their, there, they're, 168–169
Thesis sentence, 11–12, 137–138, 158–160, 183–184
Titles of persons, 41–42, 61
Titles of works
  capitalization in, 59–61
  italics for, 85–86
  of manuscripts, 95–96
  quotation marks for, 119
to, too, two, 169
Topic sentence, 127–130, 134
Transitional paragraphs, 127
Transitions, 161–162
Transitive verbs, 23

Underlining (italics), 85–87. *See also* Italics

Variety, sentence, 169–172
Verbal phrases, 35
Verbals, 35

Verb phrases, 36
Verbs, 23–24
  agreement with subject, 49–53
  auxiliary, 23, 36
  errors in tense, 156–158
  helping, 23, 36
  intransitive, 24
  irregular, 23
  linking, 24
  main, 36
  modals, 36
  tenses of, 23, 156–158
  principal parts, 23
  transitive, 23

we or *us,* 56–57
well, good, 166
who, 57–58
who or *whom,* 57–58
whom, 57–58
Word division, 84–85
Wordiness, 172–175
  in model essay, 14
Writing
  audience, 3, 5
  checklist, 6
  concluding paragraph, 138–139
  introductory paragraph, 3
  model essays, 7–18
  outline, 3–5
  paragaraphs, 127–140
  prewriting, 1–6
  purpose, 3, 5
  thesis, 2–3
  thesis sentence, 2, 11–12
  topic, 2
  topic sentence, 127–129, 133–136